SELF-DISCIPLINE

THE ART OF BECOMING MORE HUMAN

EVAN RAYMER

Copyright © 2019
Evan Raymer
Self-Discipline
The Art of Becoming
More Human
All rights reserved.

No part of this publication may be reproduced, distributed, or transmitted in any form or by any means, including photocopying, recording, or other electronic or mechanical methods, without the prior written permission of the publisher, except in the case of brief quotations embodied in critical reviews and certain other non-commercial uses permitted by copyright law.

Evan Raymer

Printed in the United States of America
First Printing 2019
First Edition 2019

10 9 8 7 6 5 4 3 2 1

SELF-DISCIPLINE

Table of Contents

Introduction 1
    Discipline as a Source of Meaning 2
    Discipline: the Ultimate Virtue 4
    Discipline: Theory Vs Practice 6
    Why this Book? 7
    Discipline for Beginners 9
    Discipline can Progress Slowly 11
    See each Moment as Representative of you as a Whole 12

1. What is Self-Discipline? 15
    Willpower is a muscle 15
    Decision Fatigue 16
    Self-Discipline as Momentum 18
    Bridging Muscle and Momentum 18
    The Row Crew Analogy 19
    Discipline and the Brain 20

2. The Different Types of Discipline 25
    Pain Tolerance 27
    Courage/Vulnerability 37
    Resistance to Temptation 41
    Tolerance for Boredom 49
    Patience 55
    Focus 66
    Initiation 70

3. The Subsystems in the Human Mind 75
  The Dopamine Reward Pathway 75
  Motivation 78
  Cognitive or Behavioural Patterns 85
  The Risk Assessment Subsystems 93
  The Higher-Self 99
  Conscience 101
  The Identity 111
  Subpersonalities 114
  Simulations of Other People 117
  You are your Discipline 122
4. Creating an Effective Team of Subsystems 125
  Finding Better External Subsystems 128
  Face-to-face Influences 129
  Content Creators 130
  Can you change the Nature of Subsystems based on other People? 132
  Unification of your Subsystems 133
  How to Eliminate a Subsystem 142
5. Self-Knowledge 145
  Commit to your Goals 145
  Detachment Techniques to Develop Self-Knowledge 148
  Writing to Improve Self-Knowledge 149
  Pushing Yourself to the Limit 151
  Listen to other People or Listen to Yourself? 152

  Mind Control and Meditation 158
6. Strength Training Principles Applied to Discipline **165**
  The Importance of Maintenance 171
  Two Goals are Sometimes Better than One 172
7. Discipline and Time Scales **175**
  Short-term Discipline 177
  Middle-Distance Discipline 178
  Long-Distance Discipline 181
8. Discipline Training Programs **185**
  Mind Control Program for Beginners 187
  Fitness Training Program for Beginners 189
  Beginner Self-Education Program 191
  Resistance to Temptation Program - all levels 195
  Improving a Specific Skill 197
  Focus Training Program 201
  Sample Courage/Vulnerability Program 204
  Perform Better at Work 207
  Writing Training Program 209
  Healthy Eating Improvement Program 213
  General Intermediate Discipline 215
  Sample Advanced Discipline Program 219
9. When Discipline is about to Crack **225**
  Remember your Second Wind 225
  Each Step Forward makes you Stronger 226
  Make it about Someone Else 227

    Remind yourself of the Difficult things you have already Overcome 228
    Use a Buddy System 229
    Become inspired by the Challenge Itself 230
    Use the Enemy Metaphor 231
    The 40 Percent Rule 232
    Be Grateful 233
    You are still Breathing 234
10. Evaluating different Discipline Techniques 235
    Daily Cold Showers 235
    Intermittent Fasting 237
    Waking up Extremely Early 240
    Orderly Habits 243
    Digital Minimalism and Social Media 246
    Relaxation Habits 247
11. The Pitfalls of Improving Self-Discipline 249
    Jealousy 249
    Perfectionism 250
    Losing Flexibility 252
12. Discipline as an End in Itself 257
Bibliography 261

Introduction

The importance of discipline or more specifically self-discipline has been well understood for millennia. Many ancient thinkers and writers including Plato, Seneca, Marcus Aurelius, and Lao Tzu have all testified to the virtue of self-discipline. However, discipline has never been more valuable than it is now.

As individuals, the greatest threats we currently face can only be combated with self-discipline. Where in the past, war, disease, famine, and natural disasters were the most pressing concerns, now we are seeing increasing threats from temptation.

Technology in general, and smartphones in particular, drastically reduce the time and effort needed to gain access to a wide variety of dopamine stimulating indulgences. Our bodies and neural reward pathways evolved over the course of billions of years where dopamine inducing catalysts like fast food, pornography, casual sex, social media, recreational drugs, and video games were either much less intense, less accessible, or entirely non-existent.

Technology giving us access to new and more intense dopamine activators is not a recent phenomenon. Sugar was first refined in India sometime around the 4th century AD and cocaine was first synthesized in 1898, both of these technological developments changed the course of human history by increasing access to the neural dopamine reward system in our brains. Where in the past these sorts of developments were either very rare and spontaneous or they were gradual as was the case when agricultural developments increased the caloric density of our food. Now we are seeing enormous transformations in our ability to hijack the natural dopamine reward system on a yearly and in some cases even a monthly basis.

In tandem with these dopamine activating temptations are unprecedented opportunities. We have the ability to learn almost anything for free or for a nominal fee. However, instead of taking advantage of this educational material many people are using the internet to access low quality entertainment.

If you were a medieval peasant living in the feudal system discipline wouldn't have done much for you. No matter how hard you worked you could have never transcended your position in society. But now, more than ever before, armed with discipline and more information than they know what to do with, people from all walks of life are turning the tables and creating opportunities for themselves and their families. Internet access is becoming ubiquitous all over the world, the main thing stopping us from improving ourselves is discipline.

Discipline as a Source of Meaning

Despite living in the most affluent period in human history, more and more people are feeling that their lives are lacking in purpose. In fact there seems to be a widespread crisis of meaning, particularly in the most comfortable and wealthiest societies. This crisis of meaning originates from one of our deepest instincts, the need for struggle.

Even a cursory glance at our evolutionary history shows that struggle has been a central part of our existence for a very long time.

Tracing back to early hominids we see an animal for whom survival itself was a constant struggle to find food and avoid predators.

Possibly even more important in the formation of our instincts were the vast array of ancestors which existed before hominids. Consistent in all of our ancestors was an intense struggle to survive, this would have been the case for our pre-hominid primate predecessors, early mammals, the amniotes which pioneered living on land, and even the first microorganisms which marked the beginning of life on earth. Our instinct to struggle has been hardwired into us over the course of more than 3.5 billion years of evolution. So what happens when we effectively transcend this struggle through the use of technology and social organization?

Since the development of agriculture, humans have become more and more effective at reducing struggle. What happens in the future when artificial intelligence makes the majority of humans economically irrelevant by taking over their professions?

There will be two main challenges.

The first challenge will be ensuring that ordinary people are able to benefit from these technological advances rather end up in economic turmoil. The solution to this challenge is beyond the scope of this book.

The second challenge will be how do people find meaning in their lives when their livelihoods have been replaced by technology? In fact, there already is a crisis of meaning in much of the world and this problem is likely to get worse rather than better in the future. The solution to the second challenge is self-discipline.

In order to find meaning in our lives we first need to create challenges for ourselves and then to apply discipline to overcome those challenges. If we ever achieve a technological utopia where people don't need to work at all and we are all living in effortless material abundance, self-discipline will be more important than ever. A lifelong commitment to discipline will be the only thing which allows us to manage our deep instinct to struggle.

Discipline: the Ultimate Virtue

Certainly, natural born qualities such as intelligence, personality and creativity are important. Intelligence, nearly as much as discipline, will decide your ability to achieve your goals in life. Unfortunately, most attempts at improving general intelligence have been disappointing at best.

While you can get better at solving certain kinds of problems through practice, that skill usually doesn't transfer over to other kinds of problems. Improving your skills in math won't make you a better chess player and vice versa. If it is possible to improve general intelligence as an adult, the process would take a long time and would require tremendous effort

Improving general creativity is possibly even less effective. While there is likely some kind of "general creative" trait, it has yet to be properly measured by psychologists. In fact, it is likely impossible to actually measure creativity accurately. Can people become more creative over the long-term? We can certainly become inspired and notice boosts in creativity over the course of weeks or months, but it's unclear that creativity can be improved as a life-long stable trait.

Whether or not personality can be changed over the long-run is still a debate in psychology as well. There is some evidence suggesting that certain treatments can produce lasting changes in personality, however, psychological theories, psychological evidence, and common sense suggest that personality remains relatively stable in adults.

Unlike intelligence, creativity, and personality, training discipline is straightforward and applicable to everyone. Improvements in one aspect of discipline will bleed over into other types of discipline. Additionally, self-discipline can even compensate for weak points in intelligence, creativity, and personality.

Discipline is a challenge we all face, no matter our nationality, ethnicity, gender, age, religion, socioeconomic status, or sexual orientation, discipline is a force which unites us. The struggle begins in infancy and continues until our final breath.

Everyday is a battle with discipline and at times we desperately want to rest and give ourselves a break, but the forces of temptation and sloth never rest, they are always trying to get the upper hand on us.

There is a movement brewing, more and more people are waking up to the fact that discipline is the ultimate virtue. Join us in the war against our inner weakness, discipline yourself so you can improve the lives of your family, your community, your country, and humanity as a whole. You are not alone in the struggle, millions of people are taking control of their lives and leading humanity into the 21st century with self-assurance and dignity.

Discipline: Theory Vs Practice

Much of the writing and general content geared towards helping people improve their discipline avoids getting too theoretical. There is a good reason for this, a big part of becoming more disciplined is done by simply "being more disciplined".

However, this book includes a lot of theory and analysis on discipline and how to increase discipline in your life. A concern when addressing discipline in this way is that readers will develop a "paralysis by analysis". I.e. a reader spending too much time thinking about self-discipline rather than actually making changes in their lives.

There is something to be said for the reality that discipline can only be achieved through action and that theory alone won't take you anywhere. Noteworthy, is that some of the most disciplined people in the world focus on action and spend little time studying psychology or introspecting.

However, if you want to reach your potential when it comes to self-discipline you would be best served using some kind of guide. As an analogy, you could go to the gym, slam weights around, and get very fit. But, having a trainer will keep you from injuring yourself and will help you reach your true fitness potential. The same goes for discipline; the theory in this book will help you avoid typical pitfalls and take your self-control to the next level.

Theory alone certainly isn't enough. The information in this book ought to be tested and refined in the context of your own life. And nothing in this book will be useful unless you make a conscious effort to improve your own discipline. In the end, regardless of how accurate or effective the theories and exercises, you will still need to execute the plan. There is no idea, person, institution, or technique which can save you except for yourself.

Some people are addicted to self-help books, self-help videos, and personal-development courses. These people are hacking their brain's dopamine reward system by creating a sense that they are making progress by simply imagining themselves living an ideal life rather than actually doing the hard work necessary to change in a positive way.

On the other hand, there are some people who consume personal-development based material that actually use the information and motivation to take their lives to the next level. You want to be in the latter group. The ideas in the book can only be understood if you actually apply them to your own life.

Why this Book?

Most people in the world of self-discipline, motivation, habits, routines, willpower, self-control, and related topics tend to belong to one of two extremes.

The first camp holds the idea that willpower conquers all. This view maintains that we can overcome any behavioural deficit through sheer self-control and any failure to act in a disciplined manner is due to a lack of moral character. This view is particularly attractive to people who have a high standard for themselves or for people who naturally have a lot of willpower. Additionally, this view is attractive because the belief itself is inspirational and actually increases self-control. When you believe that you can overcome your behavioural weaknesses using the power of your mind you are more likely to be able to do it. It is hard to argue with this view when you account for specific examples of remarkable people who transformed their lives by simply making a conscious decision to do so. David Goggins, whose life and ideas will be discussed later on in this book, is a perfect example of someone who has successfully taken this approach. Many people in the first camp are able to transform their own lives and help other people transform their lives as well. Taking on the "no excuses mentality" is undeniably effective.

The second camp tends to discount the importance of willpower or even argue that it doesn't exist at all. According to this view, the inability to follow through with goals has nothing to do with personal weakness, but rather has everything to do with environment and neurological processes which are outside of conscious control. This perspective is attractive to cerebral types who are aware of modern scientific research on self-control. The current willpower paradigm in academic psychology is that despite some ability to impact behaviour, ultimately, willpower is often overshadowed by other psychological forces.

Additionally, some people are drawn to the second camp because it leaves room for compassion for those who have made tragic mistakes in their lives. After all, if discipline is unimportant then people don't have to be blamed for their poor decisions. Finally, there are some people who are drawn to the second camp because it excuses their lack of success and their irresponsible behaviour.

The best argument for the second camp are the countless practical examples of people who attempt to change their behaviour through sheer willpower and inevitably fail. This includes changes which should be easy. Nearly everyone has enough willpower to floss their teeth every day, so why do so many people struggle with such basic habits? Also, people in the second camp do develop effective strategies to improve their lives without using much willpower at all. This usually involves changing their environment and using various techniques to take advantage of the way that the human mind works.

Despite being a cliche, the best approach is found in between the two camps. You want to acquire as much discipline as possible while leveraging the instinctual processes inside of your brain and optimizing your environment at the same time. That is the philosophy behind this book, to bridge the gap between the two extremes. In your quest for personal development there is no reason to avoid using any tool which is available to you. Thankfully, thinkers and doers in both camps can give you the tools you need to become the best version of yourself.

Discipline for Beginners

This book is a guide to self-discipline for people at all different levels in their personal development journey. Beginners may find that some of the information is unnecessarily complex and that some of the tangents are frustrating. The goal of this book is to improve your life, not to bog you down with information If you are a beginner and a section isn't relevant to your own life don't feel like you need to understand everything.

As a beginner here are your priorities in order.

1) **Build a Basic Exercise Routine:** See the Beginner Fitness Training Program in the Training Program chapter if you want more

direction. You should do some kind of strength training, stretching, and cardio. If you don't want to go to the gym there are physical practices which develop overall fitness, this includes certain types of martial arts and yoga. You haven't passed this second step until your exercise routine is a habit.

1) **Meditate every day:** See the Meditation and mind control section for more information on how to meditate. You don't need to meditate for a long time, 15 minutes is great, but if you are new you might want to start with as little as 5 minutes per day. Make sure that this is ingrained as a habit before moving onto anything else.

2) **Follow one of the Beginner Discipline Training Programs:** At this point it is up to you how you want to proceed. There are a lot of 8 week Discipline Training Programs listed in the Training Program chapter if you want some direction. Alternatively, start focusing on some aspect of your life which you know needs work. Your discipline journey is unique. There will be things which come naturally to you and other aspects of your personal development which will be more of a struggle. Over time, you will develop confidence and find that your life is completely transformed as you move towards becoming the best version of yourself.

Why start with meditation and exercise? In my previous book, *Intentional Living*, I discuss how many people think that they need financial success before they can self-actualize. For example, they might say something similar to the following statement.

"**Once I have X number of dollars I can finally do the things I really want to do.**"

This is a mistake. You can start self-actualizing right now. In fact, becoming more disciplined is the ultimate form of self-actualization.

Meditation and physical fitness are the foundation of discipline. By skipping these steps you will be building your self-control on shaky ground. If you don't have a consistent exercise routine and meditation practice you have no business trying to build a career, learn a skill, or make the world a better place.

You should put exercise and meditation in the same category as breathing, eating, sleeping or drinking. The human body can survive for longer than a month without food, but it degrades over time. The same thing happens when you don't meditate or when you skip your exercise routine, your mind, body, and spirit degenerate.

Discipline can Progress Slowly

People who are experienced improving their discipline have likely gone through a period of time where their progress slowed down dramatically. Sometimes implementing a single change can take an entire year to maintain.

If this is the case for you, don't worry if things are moving too slowly for your tastes. Instead remain patient and remember the parable of the tortoise and the hare. If you try to rush progress you might actually improve in the area you are focusing on, but other aspects of your discipline are likely to deteriorate.

When it comes to discipline, slow consistent progress should be seen as a success. However, occasionally discipline will progress very quickly. This usually coincides with a high on the motivation cycle, we will discuss this in more detail in a later chapter. If progress is smooth, take advantage of the momentum and push forward. Don't make any big commitments or goals in this state, make sure to stay humble with yourself, but you should still push yourself to see how far you can go.

SEE EACH MOMENT AS REPRESENTATIVE OF YOU AS A WHOLE

When it comes to making a disciplined choice it is easy to rationalize your way out of doing the right thing. If you skip the gym just this one time it won't be such a big deal, you can always go tomorrow. The problem with this sort of logic is that it assumes you will actually follow through. However, the person which you will be in the near future is not much different from the person who doesn't want to go to the gym right now. On any given day you could say "I will go to the gym tomorrow", but what ends up happening for a lot of people is that their plan to get in shape falls apart because they keep skipping workout sessions.

This is why it is critical to act according to principle. Living based on the principle of discipline means treating each action as being representative of you as a person. So if you act in an undisciplined way this means you are an undisciplined person. While it might not literally make sense, you can easily rationalize that you are generally a disciplined person and were only undisciplined in this one instance, but there is some truth to the idea. We can't control the past and we can't control our future, we can only control how we act in the present moment. So if we aren't disciplined right now we simply have to see ourselves as undisciplined as a whole.

It's not recommended to be hard on yourself if you slip up. Being hard on yourself can kindle negative momentum. However, you should use this idea of living according to principle as motivation to make the right choice. Before making an undisciplined decision consider the reality that this is you being undisciplined in the only time where it actually matters, the present moment.

Discipline, and life in general, comes down to the moment to moment decisions you make. Get up out of bed or stay comfortable underneath the covers. Write a few pages for your next novel or watch clips on youtube. Lace up your running shoes and go for a jog or stay inside and watch TV. These all come down to how you choose to act in the moment. Yes, long-term planning is useful and important, but even more important is learning to make the best choice right now and in the future "right nows" as well.

What do I want to be more disciplined about?

1 work
2 exercise
3 podcast
4 eating habits / drinking water
5 Relationships + boundaries
6 earrings

1. What is Self-Discipline?

Willpower is a muscle

The most widely accepted theory among professional psychologists is that discipline/willpower is analogous to a muscle. According to this view, just like a muscle, discipline gets stronger with practice. On the other hand, just like a muscle, discipline gets tired over time and needs to rest.

In this theory the more you use your discipline without resting, the weaker it becomes. Although this theory is not entirely accurate, there is a mountain of experimental evidence supporting it. One such experiment done in 1996 perfectly illustrates why academic psychologists are so partial to this paradigm. Sixty seven participants were randomly divided into two groups. Both groups were taken into a room with cookies, chocolates, and radishes. The first group was told that they could eat as many cookies and chocolates as they wanted, the other group was only allowed to eat radishes. After leading the participants into the room the experimenters left and observed through a small window. Many of the participants who weren't allowed to eat the cookies and chocolates stared at the freshly baked treats. Some of the participants actually picked up the cookies to smell them only to return them as if nothing had happened. Clearly the participants were exercising some willpower.

Both groups were then challenged to do geometry problems. Unbeknownst to the participants in the study the geometry problems were impossible to solve. The researchers weren't testing how accurate the participants would be, instead they were testing to see how long the participants would try to solve these impossible problems. The result was that participants who were allowed to eat the cookies and chocolates spent much longer trying to solve the geometry problems. The participants who were only allowed to eat radishes had to exercise their discipline in not eating the cookies and as a result had less willpower left over for the impossible math questions.

In addition to being demonically amusing, this experiment demonstrates some important information about willpower. First, it demonstrates that willpower can be depleted when exercised. Secondly, it shows that willpower is general and not specific. Solving the geometry problems relies on the same energy force as resisting the urge to eat cookies.

Decision Fatigue

Being disciplined is essentially a matter of continuously making momentary decisions to be disciplined in your actions. Pay attention to your thoughts when are struggling to do something requiring discipline, you will find that you end up having a lot of discussions with yourself on whether or not you should make the disciplined choice.

Unsurprisingly, psychologists often use the term "decision fatigue" to refer to depleting levels of willpower as "decisions" are made. In fact, the research seems to confirm that making decisions actually depletes willpower.

In an experiment, college students were shown a table with a variety of random items purchased from a department store clearance sale. The students were divided into two groups, both groups were told that they would be given one of the items at the end of the study.

The first group was given a series of choices between two items and told that their response would impact which items they would eventually get to keep. Would they prefer a T-shirt or a candle? Would they prefer a red t-shirt or a black t-shirt. The other group was instructed to simply think about all these different items, but they didn't actually have to choose between any of them.

Afterwards, both groups were given the task of holding their hand in ice water for as long as they could tolerate, this is an easily administered test of self-control. The group that had to make decisions actually removed their hand significantly sooner than the group that didn't have to make decisions. The results of this study, and a number of other studies, suggest that decision making is closely related to self-control.

These two experiments confirm the same theory: willpower is a muscle which draws on and depletes the same resources as decision making.

Essentially, what the "discipline is a muscle theory" implies, is that if you use a lot of discipline early on in the day, you will have less available as the day goes on. But, this is contrary to common sense and a lot of people's experiences.

Self-Discipline as Momentum

If you get up early, go straight to the gym, and then eat a healthy breakfast you won't be drained, instead you will be filled with energy and willpower. But, if you sleep in, skip the gym, and eat an unhealthy breakfast you won't feel great, instead you will feel burned out despite having done nothing all day.

In this book we will refer to this second model as momentum. Meaning that if you make disciplined choices you are more likely to keep making disciplined choices as the day goes on. But, if you make undisciplined choices you are more likely to continue to make undisciplined choices throughout the day.

If an alcoholic has been sober for a year it is fairly easy for them to maintain their sobriety at any given moment. But, many alcoholics will relapse into their former self-destructive patterns if they have a single drink. If self-discipline were simply a muscle, that one drink would actually make it easier to maintain sobriety because it would give their willpower a rest.

Bridging Muscle and Momentum

Ultimately, both views make sense, if you work very hard you will be exhausted and lacking in discipline as the research suggests, but if you don't work at all, you will also feel tired and lacking in discipline. So how can we reconcile these two views?

A metaphor that blends the muscle and momentum metaphors is that discipline is a person rowing a boat. In order to get started the rower has to use a lot of energy, but once the boat is moving he no longer has to row as hard to keep going forward.

If he rows as hard as he possibly can, he will eventually get tired, but if he conserves his energy he can row all day long. This metaphor reconciles the muscle metaphor with the reality of momentum when it comes to willpower.

To apply the rower in a rowboat metaphor you want to start off the day by making the right decisions, meditate and then exercise or work on some kind of creative pursuit. From there maintain a steady level of discipline for the entire day.

Yes, you can have some breaks throughout the day and this is probably a good idea for most people. Too much downtime may interfere with your momentum, but scheduling some refueling periods will actually increase your momentum because the act of following your breaks according to a plan is a form of discipline in itself.

So, using the rowboat metaphor, can discipline be trained? Absolutely yes, the more you row your boat, the better you get at rowing. You will get better at accelerating in the beginning, conserving your energy, and your endurance will improve. As you develop more discipline you will be able to maintain higher levels of discipline for longer periods of time.

The Row Crew Analogy

In addition to the person rowing a boat metaphor, there is a more complex metaphor which is also useful. In this metaphor, discipline is an entire rowing crew instead of just a single rower.

The human mind is made up of a number of different subsystems (the identity, the risk assessment system, the higher-self, etc.), some of these subsystems enter into conscious awareness and others don't. These subsystems, are just like a group of human beings, sometimes they get along, sometimes they fight, and sometimes they settle their differences.

If you want to operate at optimal capacity it is important for your subsystems to work together. If one of the rowers in a rowing crew is off tempo the boat's movement is severely compromised. The same is true with your mind, if your subsystems aren't working together your ability to execute on a plan is also compromised. In a later chapter we will discuss the different subsystems in your mind as well as provide you with a detailed strategy to help unify your subsystems.

This book references both metaphors depending on the situation. For simplicity we will normally stick to the single rower metaphor, but if necessary we will draw upon the entire row crew.

Discipline and the Brain

"The frontal cortex is arguably the most human part of the brain. Proportionately we've got more complex frontal cortices than any other species out there. It is the most recently evolved part of the brain [...] a big time frontal cortex, is virtually a primate invention where (sic) humans really running with it"

From Neuroscientist Dr. Robert Sapolsky's course Stress and your Body

The frontal cortex is divided into four parts. According to the most accepted theory in modern neuroscience three of these four parts, the premotor cortex, the primary motor cortex, and the motor cortex primarily relate to movement. The prefrontal cortex, located at the frontal part of the frontal cortex, is responsible for something entirely different.

The prefrontal cortex seems to be the center of higher-order functioning in the human brain. It has been linked to personality, the will to live, episodic and working memory, language, social intelligence, and empathy as well as qualities relating to self-discipline such as attention, planning, inhibitory control, and decision making.

According to a report published in May of 2017 in the journal Current Biology, non-allometric enlargement of the prefrontal cortex first emerged between 15 to 19 million years ago in an early predecessor to modern great apes. Allometric refers to prefrontal growth, which can't be explained by increases in overall brain size alone.

As Dr. Sapolsky explained in the previous quote, humans took prefrontal cortex development to the next level. The human prefrontal cortex not only displays higher dendritic branch complexity (neural connections) than other great apes, but is also much larger than related species.

For example, our prefrontal cortex is roughly 5 times the size of our closest relative the chimpanzee and more than 20 times the size of the prefrontal cortex of a capuchin monkey. Yes, you would expect our prefrontal cortex to be larger than our closest primate relatives simply because we have a bigger brain overall, but the important fact is that the differences between prefrontal cortex size are even bigger than what you would expect based solely on differences in brain size.

Interestingly, chimpanzees are unable to pass the 5 M&M 1 M&M test, which is a straightforward way to measure self-control. In this test, chimps are presented with two options. one of these options is 5 M&M chocolates, and the other option is 1 M&M chocolate.

The chimps have been previously taught that if they choose the larger number of chocolates, they will be given only 1 M&M, however, if they choose the 1 M&M they will be given 5 M&Ms and pass the test. No chimp has ever been able to pass this test.

A second test demonstrates that the inability to pass isn't due to a lack of cognitive ability, instead it is a problem of self-control. The chimps are presented with 1 block of wood and 5 blocks of wood. In this test, if the chimps choose 1 block of wood, they are rewarded with 5 M&Ms, and if they choose 5 blocks of wood, they are given only 1 M&M. Every chimp is able to pass the second test.

In the first test, the chimps were simply unable to hold themselves back from reaching for the larger amount of chocolates despite knowing through previous experience that this was the wrong choice. Perhaps the most important difference between humans and other animals is not our intelligence, but rather we are distinguished by our self-control.

Self-discipline and the prefrontal cortex are intimately related and are among the most human qualities we possess. When it comes to other traits very closely associated with humans, such as intelligence or culture, it is unclear how or if it is possible to improve these qualities. On the other hand, there are numerous reliable ways to improve self-discipline. This is why increasing self-discipline is perhaps the best way to become more human.

Localizing Different Forms of Discipline in the Brain

As stated in willpower expert Dr. Kelly McGonigal's book *The Willpower Instinct*, the prefrontal cortex divides up the jobs of "I will," "I won't," and "want" into three regions.

A region in the upper left corner of the prefrontal cortex is responsible for "I will" power. This is the ability to push yourself to do something uncomfortable. For example, going to the gym when you are tired, filing your taxes despite wanting to watch a tv series, or delivering a speech even though you are experiencing anxiety.

"I won't" power is managed by the right side of the prefrontal cortex. This is your ability to resist temptation. For example, saying no to junk food, fighting back the urge to insult someone, or keeping your cell phone in your pocket during a conversation.

A third region of the prefrontal cortex keeps tracks and reminds you of your greater wants and objectives. While at a shallow level, you might "want" a chocolate sundae, at a deeper level, you want to stay in shape. This third region manages your deeper wants. Interestingly, the more rapidly cells fire in this part of the brain, the easier it is for you to use your "I will" power or your "I won't" power.

2. The Different Types of Discipline

Discipline is a complicated word. People have many different associations with the term. For some people, the word "discipline" conjures up negative ideas of strict rule-bound behaviour or even worse, a heartless authority figure imposing their will.

However, these limited definitions of discipline are lacking in scope and application. As a collective, we have the ability to abandon any disadvantageous connotations associated with the word and to apply the term in the way which benefits us the most.

One reason why we need to develop our discipline is because we have a number of semi-vestigial negative emotions/instincts which gradually formed over the course of our entire evolutionary history. Although these negative emotions may prove useful in certain circumstances, they are very much overactive for the needs of modern society. Fundamentally, discipline involves transcending these emotions when it is appropriate. Dr. McGonigal's previously mentioned model dividing discipline into "I will," "I won't," and "want" is simple and demonstrates some important characteristics of discipline. However, there is also a lot of important information to be learned by dividing discipline based on the different negative feelings it needs to overcome.

Discipline is usually associated with three primary negative feelings, resistance to temptation, persistence through boredom, and pain-tolerance. However, discipline is not simply forcing oneself to eat the right foods or to show up for work every day. While these forms of discipline are very important, discipline can be defined much more broadly.

Most of the time discipline fits into one of the following seven categories: Pain Tolerance, Courage/Vulnerability, Resistance to Temptation, Persistence through Boredom, Patience, Focus, and Initiation.

Each of these different forms of discipline is applied and trained in different ways. Progress in one form of discipline will transfer over to other areas as well. The mental pattern of following through in the face of discomfort is strengthened every time you do it.

While there are seven main distinct forms of discipline, it is important to note that many activities will involve more than one of these different varieties of discipline. Additionally, the different forms of discipline are sometimes intimately related to each other. For example, an important part of focus is resisting the temptation to do other things. This is one reason why developing a certain aspect of discipline will actually improve the other types of discipline as well.

As we will discuss later on, there are also two important abilities which, despite being distinct from discipline, are intimately related to discipline. These are self-knowledge and mind-control. Both of these skills are deserving of an entire book.

Pain Tolerance

Pain Tolerance is discipline in its most primitive form. This is the ability to withstand physical pain in the pursuit of a goal. Pain tolerance, as a goal in itself, might rub some people the wrong way. However, pain tolerance is just one of the many important applications of discipline.

Overcoming pain is necessary when you begin a new physical pursuit. For example, if you start running daily after never having been a regular runner in the past, you will experience pain in your legs, feet, lungs, and possibly other parts of your body. As your body and nervous system adapt, you will develop physical and mental calluses allowing you to run without experiencing much pain at all.

With some physical pursuits, you can always induce a state of pain by simply pushing yourself to the limit, even the best long-distance runners in the world experience some degree of pain when they go for a personal record.

For many highly disciplined people, pain tolerance is not a particularly important form of discipline. Once they achieve a basic level of fitness there is no reason to push themselves any further. Maintaining that basic fitness is no longer a matter of pain tolerance, but instead, it challenges their tolerance for boredom.

Other people are especially attracted to the purity of pain tolerance as a way of exercising and expressing their discipline. Vulnerability, for example, is sometimes ambiguous and can't be measured in the same way as pain tolerance. Pain tolerance is straightforward, and for some people, it is a more reliable way to find meaning than any other forms of discipline.

 Pain, accepted voluntarily, purifies your soul

David Goggins spent his early childhood in Williamsville, an opulent neighborhood in Buffalo, New York. His family, the only black family in the area, appeared to be well-adjusted from the outside. They had a four-bedroom house, a vegetable garden in the back, and a fleet of luxurious cars.

To his neighbors, Trunis Goggins, David's father, appeared to be an accomplished businessman. He wore tailored suits and did, in fact, own a successful roller skating rink. What outsiders didn't realize was that Trunis Goggins was a sadistic tyrant who supplemented his business income by running prostitutes into Canada.

In order to cut costs, Trunis Goggins would have his family work at the roller skating rink late every night. Because they had to stay up late working, David and his brother Trunis Jr. struggled to pay attention in class.

The two brothers and their mother would regularly suffer brutal beatings from Trunis Goggins. Adding to the terror, these beatings sometimes occurred at unexpected times for no reason at all. One of the most brutal beatings occurred after David's mom took him to the clinic to treat a dangerous ear infection. Trunis Goggins didn't believe in spending his money on medical care and beat David's mother senseless when they got home.

SELF-DISCIPLINE: THE ART OF BECOMING MORE HUMAN

When David was only eight years old, his mother escaped with her two sons to Brazil, Indiana. Unfortunately, she had no money and didn't have much experience taking care of herself. After all, she was 17 years younger than Trunis Goggins and had met him when she was only 19 years old. On top of that, he never married her, so she was unable to secure any reasonable amount of financial support.

Without Trunis Goggins, they lived in poverty and after a year David's older brother, Trunis Jr., went back to live with his dad. David, on the other hand, stayed with his mom and tried his best to support her emotionally from a very early age.

In school, David found that he didn't have the academic skills to keep up with the other kids. His teacher actually recommended that he go to a special school for children who weren't suitable for regular classes. In order to stay in a normal school and avoid being singled out, David became an expert at cheating.

David and his mother continued to struggle financially, so in his freshman year of high school, they tried moving to Indianapolis, the biggest city in Indiana. Being a teenager in a new high school David's main goal was to be popular. David got involved with the wrong crowd and in his own words adopted a new "thuggish" style of dress. David's mother, unhappy with her son's new friends and lifestyle, decided to move back to Brazil after a few years in Indianapolis.

When David returned to Brazil, he experienced racism he never realized existed in his small town. As a boy, he didn't usually feel targeted based on the color of his skin, but as a 6ft 2 black teenager who sagged his pants and blasted rap music out of his car stereo things were different. David had his life threatened on multiple occasions, including a particularly frightening encounter where a stranger pulled a gun on him and his cousin. According to Goggins, Indiana was a hotbed of racism. In fact, in 1995, on Independence Day, the Klu Klux Klan marched down the main street of Brazil, Indiana wearing their full uniforms.

David Goggins had a dream of entering the air force. The problem was that Goggins was still cheating at school and no one, including his mom, seemed to be catching on. When it came time to take the Armed Services Vocational Aptitude Battery (ASVAB) Test he didn't have anyone to cheat off and failed the test miserably. On top of that, in his Junior year, he had stopped attending classes and was flunking out.

This all came to a head after 10 days of trying to live on his own sleeping on friend's couches. Just when he had ran out of money and was getting hungry, he got a phone call from his mom. The school had notified her that he was failing his classes. David came home, ate some food, and after having an honest conversation with himself in front of the mirror, he decided to grow up.

David shaved his head, started running regularly, working out at the YMCA at 5 am most mornings, and for the first time in his life took school seriously. He began tucking in his pants and avoiding the "cool" kids in his school. After 6 months of intentional study, David's reading level went from that of a fourth-grader to a senior in high school. He finally managed to pass his ASVAB test on his third try and was accepted into the airforce.

While in the air force Goggins got into powerlifting where he bulked up from a lean 175 lbs to a flabby and muscular 255 lbs at his discharge. After his discharge Goggins continued to bulk up with muscle and fat surpassing 290 lbs. At this weight, Goggins looked like a beast, but inside he felt weak. In fact, he was working night shift in pest control and was using food as self-medication. Again Goggins' life was in bad shape, not because of his rebelliousness, but this time due to mediocrity and complacency.

Goggins had his second wake-up call after watching a television special featuring Navy Seal candidates going through hell week in their Basic Underwater Demolition Seal Training (BUD/S).

The Navy Seals are the US Navy's main special forces operators and are widely accepted to be some of the most elite soldiers in the modern world. BUD/S is a mentally and physically demanding 24-week course which all Navy Seals must complete in order to move on with their training.

Rather than actually train candidates for combat, the course is mostly designed to weed out the people who don't have what it takes to be a Seal. Hell Week, the sixth week of BUD/S Training, is known to be particularly brutal. During Hell Week candidates are allowed to sleep a maximum of four hours over the course of 5 and a half days. During this period they often spend more than 20 hours per day doing physical exercises. The percentage of candidates who make it through BUD/S Training is very low, somewhere around 25 percent.

When Goggins turned on the television, the candidates were in the middle of Hell Week. He felt pathetic compared to the men he saw going through something more challenging and brutal than he had ever attempted in his entire life. Goggins was inspired and couldn't get the idea of becoming a Navy Seal out of his head.

After calling a number of recruiting stations, Goggins finally found someone who would accept him. But after weighing in and retaking the ASVAB test, Goggins had two challenges ahead of him. First, since the Navy Seals have higher requirements than the air force, he had to improve his score on the standardized test. Second, he had to lose 106 lbs in less than 3 months.

After encountering the worst cockroach infestation of his entire time working in pest control, he decided to quit his job and pursue becoming a Navy Seal full-time. By following an extreme diet and training regimen, David managed to dramatically improve his physical fitness and drop more than 100lbs. He also studied obsessively and was able to meet the Navy Seal ASVAB requirements.

David Goggins' experience in BUD/S was especially rough. Because of injuries he got pulled out of his first two BUD/S classes and actually went through a total of three separate hell weeks. He only passed his third BUD/S course by completing the last couple of months with broken legs. Instead of complaining about his misfortune, Goggins relished these experiences as opportunities to improve his mental toughness.

After becoming a Navy Seal, Goggins returned to powerlifting and bulked back up to 260 lbs. This wasn't due to laziness; his job was to carry the M60, a 20 lb machine gun as well as 6-700 rounds weighing somewhere between 40-50 lbs in total. This is on top of al the other gear that seals carry with them in combat.

When 19 special forces operators died in Afghanistan Goggins decided that he wanted to do something for their families. His idea was to run the Badwater 135 and raise money for the Special

SELF-DISCIPLINE: THE ART OF BECOMING MORE HUMAN

Operations Warrior Foundation, a charity which helps the children of American Special Forces Operators who died in combat.

Badwater 135 is a 217-kilometer ultra-marathon starting below sea level in Death Valley California, one of the hottest places on earth. The race ends at 2552 meters above sea level on Mt Whitney. Some people consider Badwater to be the toughest foot race in the world. The problem was that Goggins weighed around 260 lbs and his cardio at the time was only 20 minutes on the elliptical machine once a week. Needless to say, he wasn't ready. Also, he had to qualify for the event and the race director, Chris Kostman, wasn't very optimistic about his chances of getting in.

Kostman suggested that David prove himself in an upcoming 100 mile 24-hour race. The race was scheduled for the following weekend, so David had no time to do any training. After what he describes as the most painful experience of his entire life Goggins managed to complete the 100-mile race in 18 hours and 56 minutes.

David called and emailed Kostman to give him the good news, Kostman, unimpressed, responded with "congrats on your hundred-mile finish. But did you actually stop then? The point of a twenty-hour event is to run for twenty-four hours...". After this Goggins completed another 100-mile race and qualified for Badwater.

By the time Goggins arrived at Badwater, he had dropped all the way down to 195lbs. He was still the biggest competitor in the field, but this time, Goggins had time to train and was ready. He managed to finish the race in fifth place out of 90 competitors.

After this race, Goggins continued to pursue ultra-marathon running aggressively. At one point, while working as a recruiter for the

Navy Seals, Goggins was running an ultra-marathon every single weekend.

After years of ultra-marathons, Goggins started experiencing extreme vertigo and neck pain from running so he decided to take on a new challenge. He became obsessed with pull-ups. Goggins did some research and discovered that the world record for pull-ups in 24 hours was 4020, that works out to an average of 2.8 pull-ups per minute. Goggins was confident he could pull it off. Just like his BUD/S training, Goggins failed his first two attempts, but he finally succeeded in breaking the record on his third.

After a lot of frustration, Goggins discovered that the origin of his vertigo was extremely tight muscles throughout his entire body. In his typical obsessive style, he started stretching as much as 12 hours a day. Now he is running again, this time faster than ever, and he maintains his pliability with a two hour a day stretching routine.

Goggins retired from the military in 2015 and has since taken on a low paying job as a wildland firefighter to further test himself. He continues to run ultra-marathons and has found success in helping other people learn to embrace pain and push themselves to the limit.

In the beginning, Goggins' life was filled with pain. But, he didn't choose this pain voluntarily and became traumatized. As an older teenager and as an adult Goggins felt an intense attraction to mental toughness. He instinctively understood the purifying qualities of physical pain and sought it out through extreme tests of will.

At first, he saw the Navy Seals as the toughest people on the planet, then he discovered ultra running and found a whole new kind of pain. Goggins cured himself of his past using pain, and once he became comfortable in that uncomfortable state, he was able to find meaning through different forms of extreme suffering.

In overcoming pain, there is no ambiguity; it is the most straightforward and purest form of discipline. This is exactly what Goggins needed to cure the trauma of his youth.

Winning the War Against Pain

You will know that pain is about to deliver a knockout blow when it convinces you that the negative sensations you are feeling are so powerful that it is impossible for you to overcome them. This is a trick, understand what pain is trying to do, and eliminate its power.

In order to beat pain simply recognize pain for what it is, a signal that a certain part of your body is experiencing stress. Recognize pain as a feeling, recognize that pain exists but choose not to perceive it as a negative experience.

If you were overcome by pain, which will likely happen at some point, don't let this failure grow into a powerful momentum. Instead, quickly develop momentum in the opposite direction. If at all possible, go back and do the activity again, but this time follow through to the end.

At one point when Goggins was losing weight to become a Navy Seal, he stopped his workout 1 pull up short of finishing. After driving home, he couldn't get that one pull up out of his mind, so he returned to the gym and redid his entire workout.

Sometimes it is impossible or dangerous to redo an activity. If this is the case, find another method to get back on the disciplined path, whether that is overcoming pain or strengthening some other form of self-discipline.

Just like most negative emotions, pain is not always vestigial; in some cases, it is actually giving you valuable information. Occasionally, a painful signal means that you are injured, ill, or are about to injure yourself. In this case, you want to listen to the pain and back off.

This is where self-knowledge comes into play; it can be challenging to know the difference between giving up unnecessarily and using appropriate caution. The more experience you have with exercising your pain tolerance, the more effective you will be at reading your pain signals accurately.

Quite possibly, the most difficult pain to deal with is long term pain that you can't control. This is usually caused by some kind of medical condition like neuropathic pain or a herniated disc. When you have a sense of control over the pain, you actually perceive the pain as less intense. Long-distance cyclists often enjoy their sport, but if someone was forced to bike for 100km they would probably find it to be a very unpleasant experience.

When your pain is caused by some kind of medical condition outside of your control, you will likely perceive the pain as more intense. Additionally, some medical conditions are likely to remain with you for years if not for your entire life. The best way to deal with this kind of pain is to use the same technique which was outlined earlier. Recognize the pain for what it is, then define it as a neutral experience (not as a negative one).

Courage/Vulnerability

At first, courage and vulnerability were going to be listed as separate forms of discipline. But further analysis showed that they are essentially the same thing. This may seem counterintuitive because of the connotations associated with the words. Courage is usually considered to be a strength, vulnerability, on the other hand, is often associated with weakness. The truth is that courage necessitates an acceptance of one's vulnerabilities. The following examples illustrate how courage and vulnerability are intertwined.

- A courageous soldier entering into combat understands that he may die; this is an acceptance of his vulnerability.

- A beginner stand-up comic understands that she may make a fool of herself on stage, but she accepts her vulnerability and acts despite her fear.

- An entrepreneur risks money, time, and his credit in order to start a new business. He accepts his vulnerability and moves forward despite the uncertainty of success.

Courage is acting in a way or putting yourself into a vulnerable situation where you could be negatively impacted for the sake of a greater more important goal. The negative effect could include being embarrassed, feeling pain, or getting injured. This possibility of a negative event induces a state of fear or anxiety, which is your brain signaling that you should back off. In modern society, these fear and anxiety programs in our brain are usually overactive. This is discussed more deeply in the Risk Assessment subsystem section.

Irrational anxiety and fear strike by convincing you that what you are feeling is so powerful that you can't overcome it. Eventually you are no longer afraid of something bad happening to you; instead you become afraid of the fear itself. In some cases, this fear grows and builds on itself to such an extent that it results in intense physiological symptoms and psychological shutdown; this is what is known as a panic attack.

The way to overcome fear or anxiety is by recognizing it for what it is. In some cases, for whatever reason, we experience fear but don't want to consciously admit it to ourselves. Using your internal monologue accept that you are in a state of fear or anxiety and then redefine that feeling as excitement.

After careful introspection, you will realize that there is little difference between fear and excitement; they are both describing very similar physiological sensations. Importantly, how you define those sensations will dramatically impact your actions and your experiences.

If you are beaten by anxiety or fear don't let this become a trend. Go back and try again, but this time with more resolve. If the event has passed and it is impossible to do it over, exercise your courage/vulnerability in another way or find some other type of discipline which you can practice. Ultimately, you want to restart the momentum in the direction of discipline.

Courage has been touted as an essential virtue for millennia, and now in modern society, courage/vulnerability is more important than ever. Any time we try something new or enter into a new group of people, we are manifesting courage/vulnerability. When there are unknowns, there is the possibility of something bad happening; this possibility can produce feelings of anxiety or fear.

Fear and anxiety are useful when they are signaling a realistic threat to your physical, emotional, or financial well being. If you wake up in the middle of the night and realize that your house is burning down, fear is an appropriate emotion because it will sharpen your senses and enhance your physical strength through the release of adrenaline. Fear or anxiety can also be useful when you encounter a person who has bad intentions or are offered a business proposition which is likely to fail.

Understanding when to apply caution and when to ignore our overactive neurological fear/anxiety systems is a very important skill in the application of courage/vulnerability.

"*Man is by nature a social animal*"

Aristotle

Social anxiety, which can manifest itself in numerous different situations, also has evolutionary origins. Social ostracism would have likely meant death and/or an inability to reproduce for early humans and their pre-human ancestors.

In these early tribal groups of roughly 150 people, humans banded together using their ingenuity and cooperative ability to compensate for their relative lack of physical strength. A brief analysis of the animals which existed in the prehistoric period demonstrates that we had to contend with real-life monsters. In addition to these terrible predators, a solitary human would have to deal with starvation, thirst, infection, and other human beings.

In the past, if we didn't like the group we were connected to or if the people in this group didn't like us, we didn't have the option of leaving. In modern society, there are countless options for communities and social groups. Beyond that, if you don't like the communities available to you in your general area, you can upend and move to a new city or even to a new country.

In a tribal environment, your reputation would have been critical and doing something to jeopardize that reputation may have affected you or your children's access to resources, reproduction and in extreme situations, it could have lead to social ostracism. However, It seems reasonable to assume that people didn't experience incapacitating social anxiety all the time in tribal environments; after all, this wouldn't have been very conducive to their evolutionary fitness.

Unsurprisingly, most of us only experience social anxiety when we are with new people or with people we don't know well. A major difference between modern countries and prehistoric tribal societies is that in a tribal social environment, everyone would have known each other and depended on each other. It is common for people to experience social anxiety before a job interview. This situation is analogous to a lone human seeking acceptance by another well-established group of humans. If the lone human is lucky, they will be accepted by the new group, but they could also just as easily be rejected or even killed. The good news is that the human brain is incredibly adaptable and reverting back to a pre-agricultural perspective is more often the exception rather than the norm. If you experience a lot of social anxiety, you don't need to worry, as you gain experience feeling vulnerable in different social environments you will gain confidence, and the anxious feelings will shrink over time.

SELF-DISCIPLINE: THE ART OF BECOMING MORE HUMAN

At a higher logical level, we understand that being rejected in a single interview won't lead to any negative long-term consequences. However, we need lots of experience being rejected or at least feeling awkward in order to teach our more basic subsystems that it doesn't matter.

Whatever the source of the fear, be it social situations, business, heights, or physical injury, it is possible to acclimate yourself to this fear. The more basic subsystems in your mind are reverting to pre-agricultural function because they have no other experiences to draw upon. Once they have more experience, they will learn to operate effectively in the ultra-safe environment, which is modern society.

RESISTANCE TO TEMPTATION

In 1970 psychologist Watler Mischel led a series of groundbreaking experiments on self-control at Stanford University. Children between the ages of 4 and 6 were led into an empty room and presented with a treat, often a marshmallow. The experimenter would explain to the child that he would leave the room and return in 15 minutes. The child was allowed to eat the marshmallow if they wanted. But, if they didn't eat the marshmallow and waited until the experimenter returned, they would be given a second treat.

Some of the children ate the marshmallow as soon as the experimenter left the room others would stare at the marshmallow, touch it, kick the table, and/or close their eyes. Most of the children who were successful in resisting the temptation looked away from the marshmallow and were able to distract themselves. The children who stared at the marshmallow almost all gave in eventually. Only one-third of the children waited until the experimenter returned.

Interesting results emerged in a 1990 follow-up study. On average, the children who had resisted the temptation had higher SAT scores, lower body mass index, and higher overall educational attainment decades later.

Resistance to temptation may be a stereotypical form of discipline, but it is still a fundamental skill to develop. Essentially, it involves overcoming some kind of short-term desire for the sake of a long term goal. Temptations can include junk food, legal and illegal recreational drugs, social media, television, and movies, picking at scabs, bullying, gossip, spending money frivolously, and nail-biting.

Temptation ranges quite a bit in terms of intensity and consequences. An extreme form of resistance to temptation is when someone who is deeply addicted to a drug manages to successfully kick the habit despite the withdrawal symptoms they had to deal with. A more ordinary form of resistance to temptation is sticking to a diet despite cravings.

Temptation itself is never useful, but the desires/urges which motivate temptation are occasionally signals you ought to listen to. For example, your cravings for junk food might mean that you are genuinely hungry. However, in the vast majority of cases, these cravings/urges ought to be ignored.

Temptation attacks by exaggerating how good giving in will feel and how long that feeling will last. The way to beat temptation is to recognize this exaggeration as a trick.

Giving in to temptation might feel good for a moment, but the feeling will be much shorter and less profound than temptation would have you believe. When you are considering putting this book down to check your Instagram, recognize that Instagram doesn't actually make you feel good, on the other hand, it will put you into a hypnotic trance where your precious time disappears, and no memories are left.

Techniques for Resisting Temptation

Technique 1: Out of Sight, Out of Mind

An easy way to reduce the likelihood that you give in to temptation is by keeping the temptation out of sight and out of reach, ideally as far away as possible. Trying to get over your social media addiction? Keep your cell phone inside of a drawer in a different room. Many people already apply this technique to improve their dietary habits by getting rid of all of the junk food in their house.

The subsystems which push you to give in to temptation are usually lacking in resolve. If the temptation is right in front of you, they are willing to put in the effort to pressure you to give in. But, if giving in requires even a small amount of effort those subsystems will usually back off.

This technique works for the majority of temptations in our lives. Particularly, those temptations where the pull is low to moderate. For example, many people are constantly feeling the temptation to check their social media, but this temptation is not overwhelmingly large.

The reason why social media is so addictive is not because of the size of the reward, but rather because people have become accustomed to always having their cell phone next to them. In his book *Digital*

Minimalism, Dr. Cal Newport calls this the "constant companion model".

Here is an experiment you can try if you find yourself using social media and other cell phone applications more than you would like. Stop seeing your cell phone as a "constant companion". Keep it out of your pocket, don't take it with you when you are running small errands, and leave it on airplane mode for most of the day. If you have never tried this sort of experiment, you will likely find yourself wanting to use your cellphone in many different situations. You may be used to opening up your phone any time you have to wait for something during your day; smartphones can serve as a constant relief from our thoughts. What's interesting about this experiment is that within a few days you will adapt to living without your constant companion. You will start to enjoy the moments without stimulation where you used to rely on your cell phone. Waiting in line to buy groceries might feel boring at first, but after 10 seconds, you may find yourself deep in thought.

In fact, those short periods of boredom throughout your day are great opportunities to think about creative ideas or to reflect on your own behaviour. Constant stimulation from your cell phone will hinder your ability to think.

This experiment should prove to you that cell phone addiction is not due to the intensity of the desire, but rather due to its accessibility and the sense that it is harmless.

The technique of removing the temptation from your general area is not sufficient for more serious temptations. If you are addicted to a hard drug like alcohol or cocaine, removing it from your house is a bare minimum step.

In this book, we will learn from and adapt the techniques used in drug addiction therapy to less serious temptations. However, we will not address the specific issue of addiction to hard drugs. This topic requires an entire book in itself.

Technique 2: Cue With no Reward

An excellent technique you can use to overcome certain temptations has been used effectively by psychologists to help people defeat their drug addictions. To illustrate the method, first, we will use the more trivial example of someone who compulsively bites their nails.

While it is possible to try to use willpower directly and stop biting your nails through conscious thought, this won't work for many people. If you try to do this, you might be successful some of the time, but what is likely to happen is that you will find yourself biting your nails without even realizing it. When you feel the urge to bite your nails, bring your fingers very close to your mouth and almost bite your nails. But, at the last minute, consciously stop yourself. Repeat this pattern for weeks or even months, and you will find that you end up biting your nails less and less often.

Psychologists have used this method with crack cocaine addicts. They will have the addict go through the entire process of preparing the pipe and heating it. Note: due to legal reasons this is done without the actual drug inside of the pipe. Just before the addict is about to take a hit, the addict is instructed to put the pipe down. Some addicts who have gone through this process have had their heart rate monitored throughout the treatment. As you might expect, the first time they go through the process, their heart rate is near maximal. Even though their conscious mind knows that they won't actually get high, many of their subsystems are expecting a rewarding high. After repeating this process many times, the addict's heart rate responds less and less to the act of preparing the crack pipe.

Why does this technique work?

When it comes to temptations, certain cues become associated with some behaviour that eventually results in a reward. Renowned behaviourist BF Skinner called this the three term-contingency or the cue-behaviour-reward model. With this technique, you create the cue and go through most of the behaviour without the final reward. The reward is what created and eventually strengthened the connection. Every time the reward is withheld, the connection is disrupted.

This technique certainly won't fix every temptation. Drug addicts, for example, have many more cues than just the act of preparing their paraphernalia, e.g. certain kinds of music, particular places, and friends who are also users. However, this technique is particularly effective for temptations which bypass conscious awareness. For example, mindlessly checking your cell phone, snacking without realizing you are doing it, or automatically cracking open a beer as soon as you get home.

If the temptation involves a debate within your mind about whether or not you should give in, this technique won't solve the problem on its own. That being said, you could use the technique to gain an advantage against the temptations which occur at a conscious level.

Technique 3: Mindfulness

Before giving in to temptation, a subsystem in your mind is going to try to convince you that capitulating to the temptation will give you an incredibly rewarding experience. For example, when you are craving ice cream, a part of your mind will present eating ice cream as an almost transcendent experience. In her book, *The Willpower Instinct*, Dr. Kelly McGonigal recommends mindfully giving in to temptation on occasion in order to prove to yourself that the rewards aren't nearly as good as your anticipation would have you believe.

Choose something which tempts you regularly. This technique works particularly well with food, but you can pick something else as well. Instead of watching a movie while you wolf down your junk food, eat slowly, and pay attention to every bite. What you will find is that the actual experience of giving in to the temptation is not nearly as enjoyable as promised. In fact, a lot of the experiences and food we crave are surprisingly uninteresting. Is popcorn enjoyable without something distracting to watch at the same time? Would you drink coca-cola in an empty room?

If you aren't used to mindfully paying attention to your experiences, you may find that your preferences change as a result of using this technique regularly. You might start to enjoy different kinds of food and entertainment. Whether these new preferences are a good or a bad thing is unclear, however, the understanding that temptation is mostly about anticipation is certainly beneficial in your quest to become more disciplined.

Technique 4: Postponement

The following is another technique suggested by Dr. Kelly McGonigal. Just like the previous technique, in this technique, you also allow yourself to give in to temptation. While Dr. McGonigal recommends this technique as a default option, it is probably better to use it only as a last resort.

When you are experiencing a temptation and feel like you are about give in say to yourself "ok fine you can have the cookie/ice cream/coffee, but you have to wait 10 minutes". The idea behind the technique is that after having waited for the full 10 minutes, you often won't even feel like giving in anymore.

If you still want the cookie after 10 minutes, you can either try waiting 10 additional minutes or eat the cookie slowly and apply the mindfulness exercise from the previous paragraph. Even if you do end up giving in, at least you are developing some control over your behaviour by waiting for 10 minutes.

You can also try increasing the delay between desire and gratification to a day, a week, or even longer periods of time as well.

Technique 5: Keeping Track

Keep a temptation journal. Every time you give in to temptation, write down the date and what you did. It is embarrassing to have to admit that you messed up to yourself. At first, you might find yourself writing in your journal regularly; however, after a few days, you will be giving in to temptation less frequently. Over time you will build up streaks of days where you didn't give in to temptation at all, this is addictive in its own right. You will want to keep the streaks going and maintain them for weeks, months, or even years.

If you are trying to improve your health, but you don't want to follow a strict diet, this is a great technique. Have a list of foods to avoid and any time you eat one of these foods, or if you overeat healthy foods, you record it in your temptation journal. This way you won't be unnecessarily restricting yourself with "forbidden foods," but every time you give in, you will have to deal with the disappointment of having done so.

Why is this technique so effective?

When we give in to temptation, it is easy to rationalize why we did it or to quickly forget about it. When you write down every time you give in, you have to accept your weaknesses in plain terms. Most people imagine that they are mentally stronger than they truly are. They might guess that they check their social media accounts five times a day, but if they were to actually record their habits, that number could be as much as 20 or 30 times a day. Recording your behaviour is a method to achieve a level of self-awareness, which is very difficult to reach otherwise.

Tolerance for Boredom

Rarely discussed, however, tolerance for boredom is likely the most underrated aspect of discipline. No matter how much you love doing something, there are always moments when it becomes dull and you don't feel like doing it. Overcoming this dullness is especially important if you are trying to master a skill.

It's thrilling to watch world-class athletes compete; most sports are exciting for both observers and competitors. However, underlying this excitement are thousands of hours of repetition. There is no doubt that Roger Federer loves tennis, but at the same time, we can be sure that there were countless days where he showed up for practice despite not being in the mood. In order to reach a world-class level, Federer needs to have a world-class tolerance for boredom.

This applies to any form of human excellence, including art and science. The story behind Einstein's theory of relativity and Michelangelo's David, is thousands of hours of study and practice.

Despite the fact that ignoring boredom and plodding forward is often necessary to accomplish great things, boredom can also be a signal that you are stuck in a rut and ought to try something new. This presents two challenges.

1) First, you need to decide whether you are in a rut or if your boredom is something to disregard. You know that you are in a rut if you aren't making any progress in any aspect of your life. This includes career, health, spirituality, education, family etc. For example, you are working at a job without any long-term career prospects and during your free time, you mostly watch Netflix or browse social media instead of doing something productive.

2) If you realize that you really are in a rut, it is important to use the boredom to get out of the rut instead of giving in to the temptation to placate your boredom. In this situation, you will feel pressure to appease this sense of boredom by giving in to some kind of temptation. For example, some people will use junk food or alcohol to try to feel better.

Getting out of a rut is easier said than done. As will be discussed later, motivation cycles between high and low states. If you are currently in a rut, you are likely near the low end of your motivational cycle. Being at the low end of your motivational cycle can feel hopeless, especially if you have an emotionally volatile personality. Whether you believe it or not your motivation will return eventually. That being said, just because your motivation is low doesn't mean that you have to be in a rut, this is why you need to develop your discipline.

During a rut, instead of placating their boredom through alcohol or some other vice, some people change their lives in a drastic way to shake things up. For example, quitting their job, traveling the world, getting a divorce, having a child, or going back to school. This may improve their situation, but it might also make it worse. The only reliable way to get out of the current rut and futures ruts is to make good daily choices which develop self-discipline.

The person we discussed earlier who is working the go-nowhere job shouldn't quit just to shake things up. Instead, they ought to polish their resume and start sending out hundreds of job applications. Rather than buying junk food, they should be going to the gym or learning how to cook healthier meals. By moving in the right direction, they will strengthen their self-discipline and as a result, will have the ability to fix their situation in the future if things get dreary again.

Boredom attacks by exaggerating how bad and long doing whatever you need to do will feel. Let's say you have to write a report on a fairly uninteresting topic; boredom will try to convince you that this report will be mind-numbingly awful and will feel like a marathon. The reality is that there will likely be moments while you are writing the report where you are actually enjoying yourself and time will pass by much faster than boredom would have you believe.

Turn the Tables on Boredom by Entering a Flow State

There is a state of mind where your entire conscious awareness becomes absorbed in a single task. While in this state, nothing else matters, you temporarily lose your sense of self as well as any thoughts about other things. Imagine a computer programmer who is so absorbed by their project that they work all night long forgetting to eat or sleep. This is an extreme example of flow; people can experience flow in much shorter bursts as well. You likely have had a flow experience at some point in your life; in fact, you may experience flow on a daily basis. If you have a challenging job, you might experience flow at work, or you may experience flow playing sports. In athletics, flow is often known as "being in the zone."

Conscious awareness can be divided amongst different things and while it may be inexact, you can apply a percentage of awareness number to anything which is in consciousness.

For example, if you are eating while watching television, you might have 10 percent of your awareness on the food, 20 percent of your awareness on your text message conversation and 70 percent of your awareness on the television.

If you are driving while having a conversation you might have 25 percent of your awareness on the road, 25 percent of your awareness on the errands you need to run later, and 50 percent of your awareness on the conversation.

In a pure flow state, 100 percent of your awareness is on the task at hand. Pure flow is widely recognized as being both an enjoyable mental state as well as being an optimal state for performance. It's no surprise that you perform at your best in this state of mind because all of your focus is directed towards a single activity.

Note: flow doesn't necessarily need 100 percent of your awareness to feel fulfilled or to improve performance. Realistically, much of the time, you will be in a state approaching pure flow. Occasionally thoughts about yourself or other things will pop into your mind, but the closer you can get to 100 percent pure conscious awareness the better.

Dr. Mihaly Csikszentmihalyi coined the term "flow" in 1975 and was the first modern psychologist to investigate it seriously. While he maintains that flow can be experienced in many situations, there are some conditions which make the state more likely.

1) **You are sufficiently challenged:** If you are meant to focus all of your conscious awareness on a single activity, there needs to be enough substance to actually absorb your focus. Most people can't enter into flow driving around city streets or on the highway simply because they aren't sufficiently challenged. On the other hand, for race car drivers, flow may be necessary because any lapse in focus could spell their demise.

2) **You are highly skilled in the activity:** If you are doing something challenging, but don't have the necessary skill set, you simply won't have the means to manage all of the demands placed on you. According to Csikszentmihalyi, performing a challenging task while lacking in skill will produce anxiety rather than a flow state.

The two conditions above will help you choose the right activity for entering into flow, once you have chosen the activity here are some general recommendations you can use to further increase your chances of reaching flow.

1) **Eliminate Distractions:** Isolate yourself from anything which might take you out of flow. If you are trying to write, use your home office or go to the silent section at the library. Certain kinds of activities involve other people so isolating yourself from others isn't possible, but you can still to disconnect from unrelated distractions. For example, if you are doing sales, temporarily avoid email or communicating with anyone who is unrelated to the task at hand.

2) **Get started and commit 100%:** Oftentimes you will feel like there is no way that you can enter into flow, the activity might seem too boring at the time, or maybe you are distracted by other things. However, even if you feel this way, give it your best shot anyway. Much of the time you will find yourself in a flow state after a few minutes of effort.

There is no way to guarantee flow; all you can do is maximize your likelihood of entering the state. However, the more practice you have entering into flow, the more often you will be able to reach it.

While certain conditions and certain situations certainly increase the likelihood of reaching flow, you can actually enter flow doing anything. The state simply requires that you invest 100 percent of your conscious awareness into a single activity. As you gain experience meditating, you will find that you are able to find flow in situations you never previously suspected could be conducive to a flow state.

The most frustrating form of boredom is when you are insufficiently stimulated to enter into flow, but are unable or not allowed to do something else at the same time. For example, operating a cash register or watching a security camera.

If you believe that this is the case for you, first make sure that there is no way you can enter into a flow state. Some people hate working in a restaurant kitchen, but others enjoy it because they are able to consistently reach flow.

If there truly is no way you can enter into flow, then find an interesting activity which you can do in your own mind. For example, play chess, do math, write music, or make up stories. You might be able to come up with something useful you can use later or if not you can drop it when you leave your non-stimulating job/activity. Ultimately, this is a great opportunity to challenge your boredom tolerance. Even though the job might feel useless, you know that it needs to be done and that it is an excellent exercise in discipline.

Patience

For most of our evolutionary history, we had very little need to wait for long periods of time. Decisions and events occurred on a moment to moment basis. If we saw a predator, we would have to quickly choose between running, climbing, or hiding.

During the pre-agricultural period, whenever our human and pre-human ancestors managed to find food, they might have been able to store some of it. But they certainly would have eaten the majority of that food within a short period of time. If our ancestors had chanced upon an excess of food, storing it would usually cause problems, it could go rotten or attract other animals.

The demands of nature are immediate; there isn't much benefit to long-term planning. However, since the dawn of civilization, all great achievements have depended on individuals and groups planning much further into the future than their instincts would naturally incline them to do.

People who are able to not only think long-term, but also to act long-term have a distinct advantage in the modern economy. Unlike your ancestors, you have the incredible luxury of being able to save your current surplus in wealth. So, in the future, either you or your descendants can take advantage of that surplus. What's even more incredible is that our stored wealth tends to accumulate even more wealth, and the more we store, the more we can earn.

It's possible to understand compound interest at a logical level, but there was no similar phenomenon relevant to our pre-agricultural ancestors. Imagine one of our early primate ancestors from 50 million years ago burying 50 almonds in a hole and then showing her kids where she hid them. 15 years later, after she dies, her kids are struggling to find enough food, so they dig in the spot she showed them and find 100 almonds. This example is absurd, but the absurdity is telling. It illustrates why saving money and other forms of long-term patience are so difficult for so many people. Money and other investments often multiply in value when saved. On the other hand, most of the items and goods relevant to our ancestors either stayed the same or degraded over time. Compound interest and other concepts relevant to long-term patience often don't resonate with the way our brain evolved to think.

Based on physiological evidence, examples from modern hunter-gatherers, and in accordance with most experts in the field, persistence hunting was likely an important hunting technique for many groups of early hominids. Unlike other predators such as big cats, we weren't usually fast enough to catch our prey in an all-out sprint. However, humans, unlike most mammals, have some adaptations which make us particularly adept at endurance running. Most notably being our ability to reduce our body temperature through sweating. Because of these adaptations, early hominids were able to chase large mammals at a moderate pace until they collapsed due to exhaustion.

We don't know exactly how long it took to catch prey using the persistence hunting technique. However, in 1990 an anthropologist working with hunter-gatherers in the Central Kalahari Desert in Southern Africa observed a number of different modern persistence hunts.

The hunters were chasing Kudu, a type of antelope common in Eastern and South Africa. They worked during midday at peak heat between 39 to 42 degrees celsius. The anthropologist found that the shortest hunt was less than 2 hours and the longest hunt took 6 hours and 38 minutes. The length of a persistence hunt would certainly vary with different climates and different animals; however these numbers give us a good sense of how much patience early hominids needed. Certainly running for more than 6 hours in 40-degree weather would have required a tremendous amount of patience and determination, something very few modern humans would be willing or capable of doing.

Chimpanzees and other great apes occasionally display some basic planning for the future, but this planning is extremely primitive and short-term. For modern humans, on the other hand, planning for the future is an important part of daily life. Interestingly, humans are the only modern primates which engage in persistence hunting. Perhaps human capacity for patience and planning emerged in part due to our unique hunting style.

The patience required for thriving in modern society is quantitatively and qualitatively different from what was required in persistence hunters. Persistence hunts are measured in hours while many of the goals relevant to thriving in modern society require patience lasting years or even decades. For example, creating a prosperous environment for children could entail attending college or university, moving to a safe city or town, and then spending years building up a career/business. Another example would be saving for retirement; this requires steady, consistent, wise decisions over a number of decades.

The other major difference between the patience required for persistence hunting and the patience required for modern goals is the tangibility of the objective. A successful kudu hunt means food for yourself, your family, and your tribe. On the other hand, the modern human is aiming to accumulate more abstract concepts like wealth, knowledge, or career success. The visceral reward of catching and killing an animal will always feel more complete and fulfilling than depositing a cheque into your bank account.

It may be impossible to touch, smell, or taste our modern goals, but that doesn't make them any less important. Success no longer depends on the physical endurance necessary to hunt prey; instead, it now depends on a different kind of endurance called long-term patience.

Nearly every worthwhile goal requires acting consistently with a certain degree of restraint over a long period of time. Yes, this does require some strategic planning and various other forms of discipline are certainly important along the way, but perhaps the most difficult ability is simply having the patience to persist the entire time.

How to Improve Patience?

Now that we have established that long-term patience is unnatural and challenging, we ought to figure out how to transcend our instincts.

The first thing to do is to think back to the persistence hunt. We want to break down our larger goals into many smaller goals, and we want to make those small goals as tangible as possible.

Let's say your goal is to get a Ph.D. in economics; there are a lot of different important components to this goal making it abstract and intangible. Additionally, depending where you are at in your education this goal could take a very long time.

Getting a Ph.D. in economics involves performing well in undergraduate classes, developing intellectual relationships with professors, making a number of University applications, perhaps performing well on the GRE, doing a tremendous amount of research, and writing a fantastic Thesis. Most of these goals are still fairly abstract, and some of them require years of effort.

We could break down "perform well in undergraduate classes" even further into getting an A in specific classes like Advanced Macroeconomics, Linear Algebra, or Econometrics. However, these goals are still abstract and will require months of consistency.

The goals should be broken down all the way to the level of understanding a particular series of related concepts, performing well on specific smaller assignments, or doing a good job on part of a larger assignment. These much smaller goals are more tangible and should require about the same amount of time as a single persistence hunt.

Patience requires managing the relationship between these smaller goals and the larger ultimately more important objective. This is where the art of strategizing comes into play. How do we convert a huge overwhelming abstract goal into a series of smaller goals which make sense to our primitive minds?

Pursuing a long-term objective requires an agreement in behaviour between yourself now, yourself tomorrow, and all your future selves until the goal is achieved. Any of your future selves could interfere with or even thwart the goal entirely. If you are trying to save money for retirement, one future self is capable of rashly spending money in favor of short-term pleasure counteracting the efforts of dozens or even hundreds of other well-meaning selves. Long-term patience is the ability to remain consistent across thousands of future selves.

The best way to develop this consistency across future selves is through self-honesty and experience in committing to goals. Start off with something easy that you know you can achieve, for example, going to the gym for 30 minutes three times a week. Creating lasting changes in the appearance and function of your body takes a lot of consistency. Once you have started going to the gym three times a week, maintain this habit for a long-time, at least five years. You don't need to wait the full five years before you are ready to enhance the habit by increasing the number of times you go to the gym per week or the amount of time you spend in the gym each session. You can also take on new habits before the five years are complete. However, the point is to get used to working towards goals over the long-term. Five years might seem like a very long time. It is, that is the point. Many important goals rely on patience for periods of time much longer than five years.

The final skill to develop in improving your patience is to focus more on the process rather than the results. Achieving a black belt in most martial arts requires consistent training for long periods. Wondering when you are going to be promoted to the next ranking is not going to get you to your final goal any faster, in fact, it will be counterproductive. Attend to the process of mastering each technique rather than worrying about your status or comparing yourself to other people. You will never become a blackbelt in Brazilian Jiu Jitsu without first mastering basic mount escapes or becoming an expert at passing half guard. Some days you will show up to your martial arts class and perform well, but other days you will be tired or distracted and won't be able to concentrate fully on the task at hand. You shouldn't attach your identity to day-to-day performance; instead you are better off trusting the process, listening to your instructor, practicing the techniques, and after many years you will finally get your blackbelt.

Patience in Shorter Time Scales

Much of this section focuses on improving patience in the long-term; however, there are some benefits to improving patience in the shorter time scales as well.

Technology and industry tend to make life more expedient and more comfortable. In the past, if we wanted to eat almonds, we might have had to wait for the right season, walk over to the almond tree, collect the nuts, and crack open the hull before eating them. Now we can buy almonds in a bag ready to eat, and much of the time they have been roasted and heavily flavored to mask the subtle natural tastes and textures.

Advances in transportation technology have had a similar effect. Hundreds of years ago wealthier people owned horses, and occasionally boats were used, but walking was by far the most common form of transportation.

In the modern era, personal vehicles in certain cities and very efficient metro systems in others have made daily transportation more convenient and comfortable than ever. Ride-sharing applications like Uber are also making transportation simpler and more convenient. Much of the time, transportation is no longer even necessary because we can have groceries and other goods delivered directly to our front door.

These sorts of industrial and technological developments which improve expediency are a positive development overall. They give us much more time and freedom to self-actualize. Hours spent running errands, tending to crops, or making food into something consumable can now be spent pursuing art, science, philosophy, entrepreneurship or a whole host other mind-expanding activities.

However, the problem with removing the natural discomforts from our lives is that many people don't replace those discomforts with something challenging or difficult. Instead, they follow their natural instincts and use technology to stay as comfortable as possible. This not only atrophies their discipline, but it also makes their lives feel empty.

Individual human beings, like every other living creature, are designed to struggle against the natural chaotic forces of entropy. But, the systems that make up the societies in which we belong have leveraged the innovations of other human beings to keep us as far away from the natural forces of entropy as possible.

Perhaps the greatest threat to our patience and discomfort has occurred within the last couple of years. Fundamental to the human experience are extended periods of time without distraction. This means being alone without other people, books, movies, cell phones, computers, music, or any other stimulus created by another human being. These periods of solitude are when people wonder, think of ideas, consider the course of their own life, reflect on their social relations, make plans, and do many of the other things which are fundamental to the human experience.

For many of us, the smartphone threatens to eliminate these sacred periods of mental and spiritual clarity. Any time we feel a lack of stimulation, we can pull out our smartphones and distract ourselves with a whole host of different applications. Walking to the bus stop, on the bus, waiting in line at the grocery store, even sitting on the toilet were all opportunities to be with ourselves. Many people still have enough courtesy to keep their cell phones in their pockets while having a conversation with a friend, but as soon as their friend leaves for a moment, they open up their cell phone to avoid experiencing a moment without stimulation.

Depending on your age, you will relate to the above information differently. Widespread smartphone adoption seems to have occurred sometime between 2010 and 2012 with integration into daily life increasing on a yearly basis. This means that if you were born in 1997 or later you may have never truly been alone in your thoughts for a long period of time as you would have turned 13 in 2010 and might have gone through your entire adolescence with a smartphone. As a child, you probably didn't spend a lot of time alone as children are no longer given much autonomy before adolescence. However, if you were born in 1985 or earlier, your prefrontal cortex would have fully developed before 2010, meaning that smartphones at least didn't interfere with your neurological development.

However, there are people in all different age groups who are using their smartphones to avoid having to interact with their own minds. Also, there are people in all different age groups who are conscious of the benefits of being alone in their thoughts and are thus present enough to avoid the constant stimulation epidemic.

To improve short term patience, i.e., the ability to be alone in your thoughts, you should exercise this faculty by finding moments without distraction throughout the day. Resist the urge to check your phone when you are walking somewhere or waiting for something. Another excellent habit is to leave your phone at home as often as possible or to keep it on airplane mode. A technique recommended in other parts of this book is removing the social media applications from your phone and using them via a web browser instead. Also, consider doing a digital declutter, more information on this strategy in the chapter on Discipline Techniques near the end of this book.

If you have been compulsively using a smartphone for years and suddenly cut down your use to once every day or even less frequently than that you will experience withdrawal symptoms at first. However, after a couple of days or weeks, you are likely to have an incredible experience which you may perceive as spiritual. When you are alone with minimal external stimulation, you will suddenly find yourself fascinated by your own thoughts. You might be thinking about the course of your life, some interesting idea, the future of humanity, the nature of reality, or something else which captivates your attention. What is important about this experience is not just the experience itself, but also the implication that you don't need any external stimulation to be satisfied. The truth is that within the recesses of your own mind is a fascinating, expansive world as engaging and subtle as the universe itself.

Meditation will also enhance your ability to be comfortable in your own mind. In fact, this is perhaps the most essential reason to meditate. There is a later chapter on meditation and mind control which gives more specific instructions. The technique recommended in this book is based on observing your own thoughts and eventually finding the space within your thoughts. It is no-frills straightforward way to find peace in your own mind.

Patience and Tolerance for Boredom

There is a lot of overlap between these two fundamental forms of discipline, however, they are distinct enough to be separated.

Tolerance for boredom is the ability to persist in an activity despitenot feeling engaged or lacking in interest. This lack of interest may be temporary, for example, when you are doing something you normally enjoy but are simply not in the mood at this particular moment. With other activities you may never feel engaged.

Patience is the ability to perform certain activities and/or avoid performing certain activities over a period of time in order to allow some event to occur. What is distinct about patience is that the difficult part is the waiting; the behavioural aspect is not particularly challenging. Patience doesn't necessarily require boredom. If you are saving money for retirement, it doesn't matter what you spend your time doing as long as you meet your savings goal; from this perspective, boredom is irrelevant.

Similarly, tolerance for boredom doesn't necessarily require patience. Perhaps you are bored with your martial arts practice, but you force yourself to show up and go through the movements. After a few minutes, you will likely find yourself deep in flow and engaged in the process. In this case, tolerance for boredom simply involved pushing yourself through those few uncomfortable minutes; it didn't take much patience at all to reach a flow state.

Many activities, including meditation, involve both forms of discipline; however, tolerance for boredom and patience are still distinct abilities.

Focus

Increasing general intelligence is a holy grail in psychology. Many people claim to have a system which improves general intelligence, but further investigation almost always reveals that their claims are incorrect.

Improving your ability to focus may be the most effective way to improve your practical intelligence as an adult. Even if focus isn't intelligence in its purest form, focus can appear and function like intelligence and can compensate for a lack of intelligence in many situations.

Focus is the ability to stay on task despite the tendency to get distracted. Different levels of focus are required for different kinds of activities. While driving around town does require some focus, it certainly doesn't require all of your awareness. On the other hand, a race car driver ought to use as much focus as they possibly can in order to perform optimally.

Focus is fundamentally distinct from the other forms of discipline because distraction usually attacks below the level of awareness. Fear, pain, temptation, and boredom may, in some cases operate below the level of awareness, but they are all perfectly willing to engage in debate with your conscious mind.

Distraction, on the other hand, won't usually engage in direct conflict; instead it prefers to ambush you. If you are focusing on something deeply, distraction will wait until your focus is weak and then attack in full force with some kind of distracting thoughts, normally whatever kind of distraction you are vulnerable to at the time.

There are two main ways to combat distraction; it is important to practice both methods.

1) Maintain an intense impenetrable focus. If your focus is strong enough distraction won't be able to get in your way. This doesn't mean that you need to consume stimulants to get your adrenaline pumping; instead it is better to have a strong focus while being in a relaxed state at the same time.

2) Learn to seamlessly re-enter focus after being distracted. Unless you are blessed with a tremendous natural ability to focus, you will almost certainly get distracted at least some of the time. When this happens, relax, drop the distracting thought, and get back to work. If you have been distracted one time, it can be easy to lose your momentum because you feel like you have lost your way. Instead, recognize that distraction will occasionally get the upper hand and don't let it bother you.

In order to get better at focusing, you need to practice. The process of developing focus can be particularly frustrating because you might not notice improvements over the first couple of months. However, if you look back after a year of developing your ability to focus, you will be impressed to see how far you have come.

There are many different ways to improve focus. In this book, we will be recommending Cal Newport's Productive Meditation; however, anything which requires you to keep your attention on a complex task is a great option.

Many meditative techniques require the practitioner to focus all of their attention on their breathing, a mantra, or some other thought. What inevitably happens is that they become distracted and part or all of the meditator's attention is diverted to something else (thoughts, images, physical sensations, etc.) The challenge for the meditator is to first realize that they have become distracted and then return to the meditative process.

Productive Meditation follows a very similar approach. Choose a problem relevant to your work, ideally something complex which is genuinely challenging you. If you are a writer, you could consider how you will put one of your more abstract ideas into words. If you are an economist, you could think about the best way to visually represent some statistical data in a report. Once you have chosen your problem, go for a walk, a run, or do some mindless physical chore like mowing the lawn. Now focus all of your attention on solving the problem. Just like regular meditation, you will likely find that it is very difficult to stay on track. All kinds of thoughts will permeate through your mind. Some of them will be particularly seductive and you will want to pursue them further, resist this urge! Return to the problem you initially set out to solve. Much of the time, you won't even realize that you have become distracted by other thoughts. When you realize that you have lost focus, don't be hard on yourself, simply return to the problem you are aiming to solve.

At first productive meditation is surprisingly difficult, don't be upset if you spend the vast majority of your time distracted. However, over time, you will improve and not only will you solve important problems using this technique, but you will also enhance your ability to focus.

Note: Dr. Newport mentions a common pitfall which you may experience. Instead of working towards solving the problem, you simply rehash the things you have already established. If you are a writer, rather than actually making progress, you might repeat a clever sentence you came up with over and over again in your internal monologue.

The discussion surrounding flow in the previous section will be useful for someone who is trying to improve their focus. Focus, flow, and doing away with boredom are all intimately related.

There are a number of other techniques which you can use to improve your focus. More traditional forms of meditation are very effective and recommended for a host of other reasons as well. For more information on meditation, see the section on "Mind Control and Meditation".

It makes sense to improve your ability to focus by doing something which will benefit you in other ways. In addition to productive meditation, you could also write, learn computer programming, teach yourself physics, or learn martial arts. There is almost certainly something which will help you out in your career or personal goals, which will also improve your capacity to focus.

You can also improve your attention through things which don't benefit you directly. Some people enjoy memory challenges such as memorizing a deck of cards, and other people are able to improve their focus playing chess. If you are an experienced chess player teach yourself to play blindfold chess, this is an awesome way to improve focus.

INITIATION

Oftentimes the greatest discipline challenge that we have to face is simply getting started. Whether we are trying to get work done on our business, write a book, or go to the gym, procrastination will try to get in our way.

This force is perfectly described and analyzed in Steven Pressfield's *The War of Art*. In this book, Pressfield explains how an internal force called resistance uses all kinds of different manipulative tactics to prevent us from getting to work on what we need to be doing. A big part of Pressfield's idea is that the most difficult part of any creative task is simply getting started.

Initiation and procrastination can appear in ordinary life on a nearly daily basis. Whether you are getting up out of bed or leaving the house to go to the gym, a self-sabotaging force may try to prevent you from getting started.

There are a number of different reasons why people procrastinate. One very common reason is perfectionism. People are afraid of making a mistake, and as a result, they don't even get started.

Another reason why people procrastinate is circular and appears very odd after analysis; however it is a common reason for procrastination. When it comes to an uncomfortable activity, the anticipation is actually more painful than the activity itself. People feel this painful anticipation and mistakenly assume that the actual activity must be even worse. They end up spending hours, days, months, or even years floundering in their anticipation.

The best and most reliable way to overcome procrastination is to just do it, ignore the voice which is trying to prevent you from initiating. If that doesn't work here is a two-step process you can use to beat procrastination.

1) Recognize the activity as something which you absolutely have to do no matter what. For example, if you are a painter, don't give yourself the option not to paint. You will work on your painting at a specific time; there are no acceptable excuses.

2) Recognize that the longer you wait to begin, the more unpleasant it will be. If you just get started most of the negative feelings you are having will disappear, but if you continue to procrastinate, you will continue to feel an awful gnawing sensation about what you ought to be doing.

Unlike some of the other negative emotions, there is no situation where procrastination is good. It is always maladaptive and dysfunctional. The good news is that procrastination is one of the easiest negative emotions to overcome.

Even the biggest procrastinators are able to nearly eliminate their tendencies towards procrastination after a couple of years practicing their self-discipline. Even if procrastination feels like something you could never shake, get some practice in improving your discipline and watch your negative habit start to disappear.

COUNTDOWN TO DEATH

Writer Kevin Kelly has a macabre yet effective technique to spur himself into action. He used actuarial tables to estimate his life expectancy and installed a countdown clock on his computer, which constantly reminds him of how many days he has left to live.

It's hard to procrastinate when you have a continual reminder of your inescapable mortality on your computer screen. Could you really spend hours playing video games every day or refreshing your

Instagram feed if you were seeing your Days Left slowly disappear? Installing a countdown to death clock on your computer will be very effective for readers who procrastinate and is an interesting experiment for other people as well. Try it out for at least a week; part of the effect is watching it countdown every day.

For some instructions on how to set up Kevin Kelly's Days until Death Clock just go to this link https://kk.org/ct2/my-life-countdown-1/ or google "Kevin Kelly Countdown Clock".

The specifics of how you set this up aren't important; you don't need the most accurate prediction of life expectancy. If you are in good health 80 years is a reasonable estimate for most people. What is important is choosing a specific date and watching the days countdown. Even if the idea of this experiment leaves you with a bad taste in your mouth, you still ought to try it for at least a week. If it simply produces anxiety and you don't experience any benefits feel free to delete the clock from your computer, but you may find that the clock helps put your trivial day to day problems into perspective and forces you to focus on what really matters.

3. The Subsystems in the Human Mind

Existing within our minds are a number of different subsystems which work together to manifest our thoughts and actions. Some of these subsystems normally exist below our awareness, and others regularly enter into consciousness.

These subsystems have their own interests and motivations. They operate as individual entities. Your subsystems aren't always working towards the same aims as you, but they aren't always opposed to you either.

Just like real people in a real organization, your subsystems change their minds, have relationships with each other, and become more or less influential on any given day. There are some subsystems which everyone has, and there are some subsystems which are unique to you. Here is a list of some of the standard subsystems you are likely to find in your own mind.

The Dopamine Reward Pathway

In 1954, Olds and Milner, two researchers at McGill University, published a groundbreaking paper on the reward center in the brain. They hooked up electrodes to the septal area of rats' brains and gave those rats the ability to stimulate themselves via an electric shock by pressing a pedal. A number of different experiments revealed that the rats would do almost anything to stimulate themselves. They would neglect eating despite obviously being hungry, and they were willing to undergo harsh physical pain (walk on an extremely painful electrified floor) in order to receive a shock.

Researchers in this era had been doing a lot of experiments on the reward-punishment system in rats, but in the past, they had used food and water as rewards. With food and water, the reward effect would stop working after the rats had become satiated, however with the direct brain stimulation the rats never became satiated and would continue to press the pedal for hours on end. The researchers concluded that they must have found a pleasure center in the brain.

It didn't take long for this same experiment to be performed on humans. Dr. Heath at the University of Tulane in Louisiana surgically implanted electrodes into the reward pathway in people's brains and gave them the ability to stimulate themselves using a switch. The patients would stimulate themselves endlessly choosing not to eat despite knowing that they were hungry, and one of the patients actually became irate when told that it was time to disconnect the electrodes. Probably this experiment wouldn't be approved by ethics boards today, but understanding the research is still useful. Interviews with human patients gave us some particularly illuminating information.

The electric shocks didn't induce pure pleasure, in fact, many of the patients experienced a combination of positive and negative emotions. For example, one patient experienced anxiety because he felt like he was approaching bliss by shocking himself, but he couldn't quite get there no matter how hard he tried.

The results of these interviews are consistent with the Buddhist idea that wanting causes suffering. The participants in the study experienced a certain degree of suffering because of their desire for a more transcendent level of pleasure which the shocks couldn't provide.

Ordinary events and objects in regular life such as luxury products, addictive drugs, junk food, and social media stimulate dopamine in a similar way. Interestingly, just like the electric shocks in this study, these sorts of items produce both positive and negative emotions as well.

There is a strong drive towards consuming or buying these items, but this doesn't mean that they actually make you feel good as a whole. Sure, you might think you want to eat an entire box of doughnuts in the parking lot, but the imagined pleasure of giving in to this desire is much greater than the actual pleasure of giving in. Not to mention all of the negative feelings which would result from eating an entire box of doughnuts in the parking lot (shame, stomach pain, lethargy, etc.).

The dopamine reward pathway is an important and influential subsystem in our mind. Its job is to guide our behaviour through reward or contrarily, to guide our behaviour through the absence of reward, which is effectively punishment.

The Buddhist idea of Nirvana is to reach a state where you have transcended your dopamine reward system and are no longer beholden to its whims. Although this is an interesting solution, it is not the recommendation given in this book. Instead, the alternative is to integrate the dopamine reward system into a rational functional unified series of subsystems.

The dopamine reward pathway can be extremely influential on our behaviour. It is important to recognize its influence, temper this influence when it is misguided, and take advantage of the influence when it is pointing us in the right direction.

Earlier we discussed how the dopamine reward pathway encourages us to do all kinds of nasty things like eating junk food or using addictive drugs, but it can also make us do things which are in our interest as well, such as going to the gym, showing up for work, or practicing an instrument. In fact, the majority of our behaviour is in some way mediated by the dopamine reward system.

If you are feeling a strong inclination towards a behaviour which is in your best interest in the long-run then use that momentum and allow your dopaminergic pathway to guide your behaviour. However, if you are feeling a strong inclination towards a negative behaviour use the recommendations in the section on Resistance to Temptation: become aware of the desire, recognize that giving in won't bring you any kind of lasting or transcendent happiness, and then let the desire go rather than try to fight it.

Motivation

Motivation is a force which can either increase or decrease our capacity to overcome certain kinds of discomfort. Yes, we can use motivation to get things done, but the problem is that it is unreliable. Some days you will feel motivated, other days you won't.

Discipline, on the other hand, doesn't depend on how you feel. Discipline allows you to do what needs to be done whether you feel like it or not. Motivation is great when it's there, but when you aren't feeling motivated it is important to have enough discipline to hold the line.

Motivation follows an ebb and flow cycle.

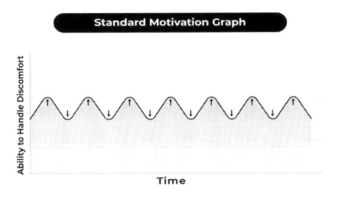

This graph shows how motivation affects your ability to overcome discomfort across time. Some days you will feel good, and as a result, you will be able to accomplish a lot, other days you will lack in motivation and will unable to perform at the same level. People who rely on motivation are depending on a force largely outside of their control. The ebb and flow of motivation isn't necessarily as uniform as it is in this graph. Occasionally the high or low point will reach greater extremes or will last longer. However, the essential point behind the graph still stands.

Above is an example of someone who is increasing their discipline over time. Everyone is subject to the ebb and flow of motivation, but this does not mean that your capacity to overcome discomfort is outside of your control. Instead, if you work at improving your discipline over time you will get better and better at overcoming discomfort despite the natural cycle of motivation.

Sometimes you will hear people complaining about not having the motivation to do the challenging and important things that they really want to do. This way of thinking is not productive. While it is possible to get yourself energized by watching a motivational video on youtube or reciting affirmations, you can't always control your motivation, some days you will just feel terrible. It's not prudent to rely on motivation to get things done; rather discipline is the force you can depend on when your motivation is low.

Emotional Stability and Motivation

Motivation is deeply related to emotionality. Someone who is very emotional is likely to cycle between states of extreme motivation and feeling like they have no motivation at all.

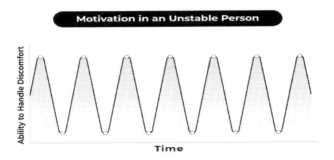

Above is an example of an extremely emotional person, notice the pronounced highs and lows in their ability to overcome discomfort.

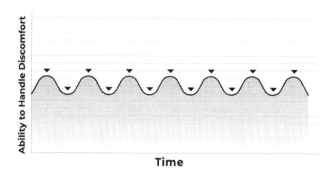

The above graph displays the motivation cycle of a more emotionally stable person. There is very little difference between their high and low states.

In the context of developing discipline, emotional stability doesn't impact the importance of becoming more disciplined over time. Whether you are emotionally stable or not you should still try to become as disciplined as possible.

An interesting implication of these graphs is that when it comes to motivation, there might be some benefit in being emotionally unstable, after all, the emotionally unstable person has higher highs. An emotionally unstable person might have greater potential for creative tasks which benefit from intense levels of inspiration.

On the other hand, when it comes to tasks which require consistency, which is the case for most jobs. It is better to be emotionally stable. A police officer, a lawyer, or an accountant can ruin their career with one big mistake. While an artist, on the other hand, can create something remarkable with one moment of inspiration.

Understanding the ebbs and flows of your motivation graph could help you choose between a job involving a lot of responsibility or a job involving creativity.

Dealing with the Highs and Lows

Counterintuitively, the high points of motivation can be more dangerous than the lows. While motivation is an extremely powerful force which ought to be used alongside discipline, it can cause people to overreach. When you are in a motivated state, it is easy to imagine that you will remain in that state indefinitely. So it is tempting to set goals or to make commitments which depend on you remaining in that motivated state. For example, you might start a business which requires a level of effort you can't maintain along with all the other obligations in your life.

Don't set any goals while you are extremely motivated and don't create any goals when you are unmotivated either. Try to set your goals when you are in a neutral and contemplative state; this is usually when your motivation is in the middle range. In this state, you will be able to create interesting, realistic, but also challenging goals which will take your discipline to the next level.

In extreme cases, people make terrible decisions in a highly motivated state. This can include irresponsible business investments, excessive spending, gambling, having sex with the wrong people, binge drinking, and dangerous drug use.

If you tend to make bad decisions when your motivation is high, the best thing you can do is to recognize the state that you are in. Simply being aware of the fact that you are on a motivational high will help you avoid doing something you will regret later. If your motivation is high channel this into something productive, you will be amazed at what you are capable of doing.

When your motivation is low it can be hard to imagine that it will ever return to a normal state again. But, no matter how you feel, your motivation will return to normal eventually. In the meantime, make sure that you maintain all of your goals and obligations. You don't need to hit any personal records, but keep going to the gym. Your meditation sessions might feel terrible, but do it anyway. If you are writing a book, keep hitting your daily word count no matter how difficult it is to get the writing to flow. Hitting your minimum standards on a low will give you a stronger foundation for when your motivation returns. Additionally, maintaining your minimum standards will make the low much more tolerable. If on the other hand, you let things slide while your motivation is low, you will feel worse, and your discipline will atrophy.

Triggering Motivation

Chasing motivation is often an unnecessary and potentially fruitless pursuit. If you don't bother with chasing motivation, it will return anyway. And sometimes no matter how hard you try, you can't pull yourself out of an unmotivated state. That being said, being extremely unmotivated can make it very difficult to accomplish the things you know you should be doing. Triggering motivation often works. The challenge is understanding your own triggers.

A motivational trigger is a phrase, an emotion, a thought, an audio clip, a video, or any other stimulus which helps you reach a motivated state. Some very common triggers are thinking about your mortality, your children, or your ambitions.

The odd thing about motivational triggers is that they might work for years and then one day they suddenly stop working. Motivational triggers can be overused; in this case, you develop a tolerance to that specific trigger over time. In other situations, you will outgrow a trigger. Finally, in certain cases, your motivation simply won't increase no matter which trigger you use.

Overall, triggering motivation is a very personal endeavor. What works for someone else won't necessarily work for you. Don't be surprised if you struggle with triggering your motivation, it is an inexact science, and no one has 100 percent control over their motivation's ebbs and flows.

Cognitive or Behavioural Patterns

A cognitive or behavioural pattern is a response to a stimulus which manifests itself through thoughts, feelings, or behaviours.

An example of a cognitive or behaviour pattern is an anxiety response to a hypodermic needle. Some people respond to the possibility of an injection with an extreme internal sense of anxiety and in certain cases physical displays of anxiety as well.

Another example of a behaviour pattern would be drinking a cup of coffee or brushing your teeth first thing every single morning. These very basic subsystems are deeply entrenched in many people's minds.

A common cognitive pattern would be immediately thinking positive thoughts anytime someone you like is mentioned in conversation.

Optimizing your cognitive and behavioural patterns means encouraging the patterns which make your life better and eliminating the patterns which are maladaptive. Going to the gym first thing after work is a superior behaviour pattern compared to going home, cracking open a beer and watching TV. Fortunately, anyone is capable of transforming their cognitive and behavioural patterns. Even if you are currently living a dysfunctional life with poor habits and almost no discipline you are capable of becoming much more than you might think is possible.

Habits

Habits are an important kind of behavioural pattern which work synergistically with a well-developed self-discipline. When you do some challenging task regularly, ideally at the same time every day, it becomes easier and easier to do. Overtime it requires almost no discipline. In the beginning that behaviour may require some discipline to implement, but after reaching habit status, it will happen more naturally. Strong behaviour patterns help you develop momentum throughout the day. When you stick with these habits, they put you on the right track and make further disciplined choices easier.

On the other hand, breaking strong behaviour patterns can slow down your momentum. If you normally get up early and exercise, but one day you sleep in and skip the gym it will likely be more difficult to apply your discipline later on in the day.

The goal is to create a set of beneficial and productive habits rather than negative dysfunctional habits. The logical approach is to use discipline to add new behaviours in the beginning and to continue to apply discipline until the behaviour becomes a habit.

Alternatively, if you are trying to eliminate a negative habit, you can use a very similar model. Apply discipline in the beginning and continue to use as much discipline as is necessary until the habit is eliminated.

Strong habits include meditation, an exercise routine, strong performance at work, healthy eating, consistent sleep, and self-education. Negative habits include unnecessary personal conflict, regular drug and alcohol consumption, watching television every day, compulsive social media use, and regular consumption of junk food.

It is best to add one or two new habits at a time. However, if you choose to add two new behaviours at the same time, make sure that they belong to different categories. For example, add 15 minutes to your daily run in the morning and read fiction before going to bed every night. Notice that one of these behaviours is physical, and one of them is cerebral, this is ideal.

Avoid adding two behaviours which belong to the same category. For example, it would be a bad idea to try to add 15 minutes to your daily run in addition to adding two gym sessions per week.

One situation where it is acceptable to add two very similar behaviours is when you are training for a specific goal and need more drastic implementations to meet your objective. For example, if you are training for a sports competition, it might make sense to add two fitness habits at the same time.

Another type of behavioural change is an "I won't" change (I won't bite my nails, I will stop drinking coffee, I will stop eating fast food after work), "I won't" changes pair up well with "I will" changes (I will go to the gym, I will read, I will meditate).

New behavioural patterns stress your discipline more than anything else. The problem with adding more than two behaviours at a time is that your discipline is likely to become overworked. Either you will not implement the behaviours correctly, or other aspects of your life will be negatively impacted because you won't have enough discipline left over to maintain the rest of your positive habits.

Sometimes you will hear people give a definite number in terms of how long it takes to develop or break a habit (1 week, 21 days, 66 days). These numbers are arbitrary. The truth is that habits continue to develop over time, and there is no particular day where a new behaviour transforms into a habit. The more time you consistently maintain a behaviour pattern, the less discipline is required to continue maintaining it. Also, the more time you avoid some particular behavioural pattern, the easier it is to continue avoiding it. Certain behaviours become more entrenched more quickly, and certain people are able to develop habits faster than others. Ultimately, habits are a continuum and not a category. Although both are habits, there is a big difference between a habit you have maintained for a month and a habit you have maintained for years.

Atomic Habits

In October of 2018 popular blogger and productivity expert James Clear published his influential book, *Atomic Habits*. The word Atomic is an intentional double entendre. It can refer to something very small, in this case, a very small habit. But, the word Atomic can also refer to having a massive impact. With this title, *Atomic Habits*, James Clear is pointing out how a lot of tiny changes summed together can produce a life-changing effect.

Clear developed a four-part process which characterizes the development of any habit, negative or positive.

1) Cue - Stimuli in the environment which triggers the habit.

2) Craving - Desire for some kind of effect.

3) Response - Action, the habit itself.

4) Reward - End goal of the habit.

James Clear acknowledges the similarity to behaviourist BF Skinner's "stimulus, behaviour, reinforcement" theory. There is a direct one-to-one relationship between three of the elements in Clear and Skinner's models: Cue is similar to stimulus, response is similar to behaviour, and reward is similar to reinforcement.

"Craving", on the other hand, is an additional element which doesn't match up with any aspect of Skinner's model. However, the idea of a "craving" being important in understanding human action is something which likely wouldn't have appealed to Skinner's behaviourist colleagues. After all, the behaviourist paradigm discounted the importance of mental phenomenon, it focused instead on behaviour as the name suggests.

Based on this clever four-part model, Clear creates and then elaborates on two systems. One system for creating positive habits and another system for eliminating negative habits.

Creating positive habits:

1) **Make the cue obvious:** If you want to read more, leave books in places you will see throughout the day. If you want to floss every day, make sure that your floss is easily visible in the bathroom.

2) **Make it more attractive - increase the craving:** Clear suggests taking advantage of the fact that you develop similar desires to the people close to you and the cultures you are a part of. If you want to get in shape, join a group of people whose main goal is to do the same thing. If you want to meditate more often, befriend people who regularly meditate.

3) **Make the response easy:** Instead of trying to meditate for an hour every day, simply meditate for a minute every day. Instead of folding your laundry, fold one pair of socks. Admittedly this is a bit extreme. Much of Clear's book is about succeeding using minimum willpower, which is a problem. People should be increasing their discipline and improving their habits at the same time. Ultimately, his essential point is correct, start with something easy and work up. However, there is no reason why people with some basic self-discipline can't fold all of their laundry in one go or start by meditating 15 minutes a day.

4) **Make the reward more satisfying:** Use habit trackers to take advantage of the feeling of progress. Trying to run every day? Mark an X on the calendar each time you follow through. After a couple of weeks, you will develop a chain of Xs, and each time you put down a new X, you will feel a small sense of accomplishment. You won't want to break the chain, and this will motivate you to stick to your goal.

Eliminating negative habits:

1) **Make the cue invisible:** Want to avoid using social media? Leave your phone in another room. Trying to stop drinking? Avoid people and situations which make you want to drink.

2) **Make it unattractive - kill the craving:** Clear recommends reframing your mindset when it comes to craving a negative habit. Many people have an unproductive mindset when it comes to alcohol. They feel like they need alcohol to socialize or that they need alcohol to enjoy their evening. By reframing this mindset and understanding that they can socialize without alcohol and that they don't actually need alcohol to enjoy themselves, they will reduce their craving substantially. This is similar to the technique suggested earlier in this book in the resistance to temptation section. Recognize that giving in to temptation is usually not as satisfying as your dopamine reward pathway would have you believe.

3) **Make the habit difficult:** Many people do this naturally when it comes to food; they simply don't keep unhealthy food in their house. On the other hand, if you tend to spend too much money leave your credit card and the majority of your cash at home.

4) **Make the reward unsatisfying:** Create a punishment for giving in. For example, if you compulsively bite your nails get a nasty

tasting nail polish. Another way to make the reward unsatisfying is to ask someone to be your accountability partner if your discipline caves in you have to tell them. This way, you will feel embarrassed if you ever fail to resist temptation.

In addition to the above systems, James Clear makes use of SJ Scott's Habit Stacking widely throughout his book. This is a simple, but brilliant way to implement a new habit into your routine.

Take something you already do every day and then pair your new habit on top of that. For example, let's say you drink coffee first thing in the morning, make it a habit to start writing as soon as you take your first sip of coffee. Another example would be preparing a salad as soon as you take off your work clothes. Habits form more easily, and they are more robust when they are performed at a specific obvious time or in a particular situation. Habit stacking is effective because there is no ambiguity, you know exactly when you are supposed to act.

Atomic Habits is a useful book; however, there is one essential problem. Clear believes that self-discipline as a force is so weak and ineffectual that he essentially ignores its value in creating habits. The truth is that many people have weak discipline, but the main reason why is that they never bothered to train it. That being said, because he believes that willpower doesn't really work, Clear needs to focus entirely on other techniques. As a result of this constrained thinking, he has to be very creative in his new tactics. On the other hand, people who rely more on their discipline sometimes miss clever opportunities to improve their approach because they know that they can power through almost anything.

The best strategy is to use the sorts of techniques Clear recommends while acquiring discipline at the same time. Discipline and habits are not opposing forces; rather they complement each other perfectly.

THE RISK ASSESSMENT SUBSYSTEMS

Your Risk Assessment System is a collection of mini-subsystems in your mind which regularly evaluate the likelihood and potential danger of different events. They assess both events within your control and events outside of your control as well. Nearly any event which could affect you at some level is assessed by the risk assessment system.

Unfortunately, this system is usually overactive for the safe environments which one tends to interact within most modern societies. This is no surprise after all the risk assessment subsystems were created over the course of billions of years of evolution in countless different perilous environments.

Hunger, for example, evolved across billions of years in species which oftentimes struggled to find the bare necessary amount of calories needed to survive. You, on the other hand, have likely never truly been at risk for starvation.

In the developed world and much of the developing world as well, people are more likely to suffer from health problems relating to obesity rather than insufficient calories. In fact, a study published in 2016 investigated BMI levels across 200 countries between 1975 and 2014. The researchers found that in 2014, around 13 percent of the global population was obese, while only 9 percent of the global population was underweight. Additionally, the authors predict that this gap will continue to increase. Note: underweight means a BMI below 18.5, and this certainly doesn't imply starvation.

That being said, the risk assessment subsystems are not entirely vestigial. Hunger, when correctly calibrated, can indicate when we truly ought to consume food. Additionally, the modern environment in which we find ourselves is not entirely risk-free. While we still do face some physical dangers, as mentioned earlier in this book, the greatest dangers we face are related to temptation.

Our challenge is that the risk assessment subsystems are designed for extreme life-threatening events, for example, natural disasters, predators, starvation. They don't lend themselves well to junk food or social media addiction.

Interestingly, there have been some attempts to activate the risk assessment system in response to these modern threats. Look at cigarette packaging almost anywhere in the world; the imagery is so macabre that the photos themselves even disturb non-smokers. Or consider the way that certain illegal drugs have been depicted as "burning holes in your brain." In a literal sense, these are cartoonish and almost offensive exaggerations. In general, responsible use of almost any illegal drug at reasonable dosages will cause minimal to no side-effects.

But, taking a literal view of the facts surrounding addictive drugs and modern temptations, in general, might be missing a deeper reality. Perhaps the potential addictive quality of cigarettes and other drugs is so terrible that we ought to make use of our cartoonish exaggerated risk assessment system.

The question of whether or not you should apply the risk assessment subsystems to modern temptations is an individual matter. Due to our psychological and neurological make-up, we respond very differently to different temptations. Some people are able to have one or two alcoholic drinks and call it a night, other people are alcoholics for whom a single drink will trigger a nasty self-destructive streak. Understand which temptations you can handle and which temptations you can't. For the temptations you can't handle feel free to apply the associated risk assessment subsystem, this will help you avoid ever giving in again. For the other temptations which you want to continue using in moderation, you will need to apply discipline and habit to keep your use in check.

IMPROVING YOUR RISK ASSESSMENT SUBSYSTEMS

Having a well-developed risk assessment system gives you the freedom to pursue activities which aren't particularly risky but appear dangerous to the more primitive parts of your brain. Some examples include: paragliding, airplanes, dentists, vaccines, or small spaces

Another reason why you want to improve your risk assessment subsystems is that if you push your discipline to the limit, particularly through physical pursuits, many times it is helpful if the associated risk assessment subsystem is well developed. For example, if you are running an ultra-marathon it is important to understand the difference between extreme discomfort and potential for physical injury.

Having effective risk assessment subsystems will not only keep you safe when pushing your discipline to the limit. But, it will also give you the confidence needed to push your discipline further than you would otherwise feel comfortable doing.

As mentioned earlier, the risk assessment system is usually overactive. However, there are certain kinds of situations where the risk assessment is actually underactive.

Much of the malfunctions are associated with a well established cognitive bias called the availability heuristic. This a mental shortcut which nearly everyone uses consciously and unconsciously to some extent. The availability heuristic involves assessing the likelihood of an event by how easily examples of that event are brought into mind.

It's easy to think of specific examples of plane crashes, shark attacks, or terrorist attacks despite the fact that these are all very uncommon events. Even if you understand this fact that these events are extremely unlikely, your risk assessment subsystems may become activated and induce a fight or flight response.

This fight or flight response can make people avoid doing things like getting on airplanes despite knowing that the likelihood of an accident is extraordinarily low. On the other hand, many people's risk assessment subsystems don't activate when it comes to genuinely dangerous behaviours such as texting/drinking and driving. Some people avoid these genuinely dangerous activities because their rational mind is able to control their behaviour. Other people need a strong emotional reaction from their risk assessment subsystems in order to overcome the inconvenience of finding a different way home.

The goal should be to divorce the availability heuristic from your risk assessment subsystems and to replace it with your rational calculations. This is much easier said than done and you will likely need to work through each of your malfunctioning risk assessment subsystems individually through exposure. Even if you consciously understand that something isn't actually dangerous, that knowledge alone won't necessarily stop your risk assessment subsystems from activating. Instead, you need to show your risk assessment subsystems that whatever it is that they fear is not actually dangerous. For example, if you have severe social anxiety, this means that your risk assessment subsystems are grossly exaggerating the likelihood of some kind of embarrassing event occurring and as a result, they are activating inefficiently. The way to overcome this fear is by exposing yourself to various social situations and showing your risk assessment subsystems that embarrassing events are actually quite uncommon. This could include asking strangers for the time, starting up conversations with strangers in different environments, attending formal and informal social events where you don't know anyone, joining clubs, etc.

As you expose yourself and your risk assessment subsystems to these various different social situations, they will respond more and more appropriately over time. Not everyone needs a targeted training protocol to improve their risk assessment systems. Risk assessment subsystems will learn through experience. A special exposure program administered on your own or with the help of someone else is better reserved for more extreme situations. If over the course of your life, you simply don't allow your risk assessment subsystems to control your behaviour in an irrational way, their effect will be diminished. Get on the airplane, attend the social gathering, accept the public speaking gig, or willingly go into small spaces such as the MRI machine.

By making it a general habit to ignore your risk assessment subsystems when they are malfunctioning they will learn to improve over time. If, on the other hand, you give into your risk assessment subsystems when you know that they are sending you irrational signals, they will gain power over you and send you more and more absurd, nauseating, and incapacitating messages.

Meditation, among its many benefits, improves risk assessment system function. It increases the influence of you (your discipline) and that of your higher-self, while decreasing the influence of your risk assessment system. The risk assessment subsystems become overactive in a state of mental chaos. Meditation creates mental order, which makes the risk assessment subsystems more timid and less capable of unwanted influence.

Consulting your Risk Assessment System

There are times when you need to know the potential dangers associated with making different choices. In this situation, you usually want to communicate with the appropriate risk assessment subsystems. The challenge with communicating with your risk assessment subsystems is that they often make mistakes. However, when you are in a state of mental and physiological order, the risk assessment subsystems can actually be very effective. The following will put you into the ideal state for communicating with your risk assessment subsystems. This process will take some time, if you are in a rush you can skip to step four.

1. Take care of any physiological needs. Go to the bathroom, drink some water, eat a snack. A strong physiological urge can interfere with your risk assessment system's ability to function.

2. Go for a short walk or do some pushups. Light exercise can make you feel more relaxed and clear your mind.

3. Disconnect from social media and find a way to isolate yourself from other people for at least a few minutes.

4. If you have a meditation practice, you can do that. Otherwise, slow down your breath and become aware of each inhalation and exhalation.

Sometimes it is difficult to enter into a state of mental and physiological order, especially if you have been stressed out all day. However, the above four steps should be able to help you relax.

Once you have established a state of mental and physiological order, you want to start communicating with your risk assessment subsystems. The best subsystem for communicating with your risk assessment system is your higher-self. If you don't have a strong connection to your higher-self, you can always communicate with your risk assessment subsystems directly. Even if you follow all of the steps properly you still might not get accurate information from your risk assessment subsystems. Whatever the case may be, it is best to communicate via your higher-self, but if this isn't possible, then at least try to evaluate the situation rationally.

The Higher-Self

Our higher-self is a subsystem which is representative of the best version of ourselves. Many people have had the experience of knowing what ought to be done, but choosing to do something else anyway. This means that they have chosen to ignore their higher-self.

- The higher-self is not beholden to emotions or short-term thinking.

- The higher-self is not influenced by the ego or the desire to feel superior.

- The higher-self balances responsibility to society, responsibility to family, and responsibility to self.

- The higher-self thinks in terms of long-term growth.

- The higher-self understands the importance of balance and conservation.

- The higher-self is unaffected by hedonistic or sensual desires. However, when hedonistic or sensual desires serve your greater long-term interest your higher-self will not hesitate to encourage them.

Not everyone is in contact with their higher-self; however it is always possible to communicate with your higher-self. The challenge is not simply communicating, rather the hard part is actually listening to what it has to say. Often the recommendations are contrary to your short-term desires. This is where discipline comes into play. After listening to your higher-self, apply your discipline to implement its suggestions.

The higher-self is not always correct in its assessments. However, it is the best version of you. As you gain knowledge and experience your higher-self will gain knowledge and experience as well. Your higher-self's understanding will always be the best understanding that you can manage.

Your higher-self usually communicates with you directly, primarily through words and ideas. However, it may communicate with you indirectly using images, emotions or other methods.

Your higher-self doesn't like to debate. If your higher-self sends you a message you can debate what it says amongst your other subsystems and decide whether or not it is correct (it usually is), but don't expect your higher-self to get involved in the discussion. Actually, if you want to test to see whether you are communicating with your higher-self or a different subsystem try arguing with it. Most of your subsystems are up for a debate, your higher-self is an exception in this regard. If the subsystem argues back you are probably communicating with your conscience or your identity.

Note: Many people experience strange coincidences or symbolic events in the external environment and interpret this as their higher-self communicating with them; this interpretation is a mistake. Your higher-self exists solely within your mind. Misinterpreting events in the external environment as being signals from your higher-self is a barrier to self-knowledge.

Conscience

Most people have a conscience subsystem which keeps them behaving in righteous ways even when no one else is judging them. Freud referred to the conscience as the superego and saw it as a fundamental part of the human personality.

The conscience is a police officer operating in your mind who's legal code is based on your own morality.

Our own moral codes develop through a complex interaction of our thoughts, experiences, genetics, family, and the morality of the society(ies) in which we are a part. Our conscience doesn't choose our moral code; instead it is a system which enforces it.

Conscience influences different people to a greater or lesser extent. Some people will only feel the deterring effects of conscience before committing the most heinous moral acts. For example, they might lie, cheat, litter, manipulate, and/or generally disrespect other people, but they still have strong reservations against violence and theft.

On the other extreme, a substantial minority of people are in a constant conversation with their conscience. Some martial artists bow before stepping onto the mat even if no one else is watching. Other people dedicate nearly every waking moment to helping their community.

The vast majority of people exist somewhere in between. While they may occasionally lie for their own benefit or commit some other immoral act it's usually not grievous and their conscience is likely to scold them later.

As your discipline improves, you will find yourself listening to your conscience in more and more situations. You probably don't steal or cheat people out of their money, but you might do more subtle things which your conscience is trying to get you to stop doing. For example, maybe you have a bad habit of constantly teasing a particular friend even when it isn't funny or maybe you haven't visited a physically immobile friend/family member in over a year.

SELF-DISCIPLINE: THE ART OF BECOMING MORE HUMAN

Neither of the above examples is morally repugnant, and these kinds of minor offences to conscience are commonplace. Why don't you visit your physically immobile friend/family member more often? Because it is more convenient and comfortable not to do it. This is why disciplined people are more likely to listen to their conscience; they are able to find a way to overcome those inconveniences and do what they know they ought to do. Self-discipline doesn't necessarily make your conscience more powerful; rather it simply gives you the resources to do what it says.

People Without Conscience

There is a small minority of people who don't have a conscience subsystem at all. These sorts of people are known as sociopaths or psychopaths.

There is debate among psychologists as to the specific definitions of sociopathy and psychopathy as well as the question of whether there is a difference between the two personality disorders. In this section, we won't be concerned with the theoretical debates among psychologists; instead we will focus on what is actually known about people without a conscience subsystem.

According to Dr. Robert Hare, a widely recognized expert on psychopathy, around 1% of the general population meets the criteria for psychopathy based on his checklist. However, the rate of psychopathy among criminals and prisoners has been shown to be substantially higher than 1%.

People without conscience have been described as interspecies predators, taking advantage of the ordinary person's tendency towards cooperation and agreeability.

While conscience exists as one of the fundamental subsystems like the dopamine reward pathway and the risk assessment system, psychopaths demonstrate to us that it is distinct from the other fundamental subsystems because it doesn't exist universally in everyone's mind.

At rest, sociopaths display substantially less metabolic function in their prefrontal cortex, the part of the brain which is responsible for self-discipline as well other higher-order functions. Interestingly, when asked to perform an activity requiring self-control, for example walking backwards quickly, sociopaths display more metabolic function in their prefrontal cortex. Arguably, this suggests that it requires more effort for sociopaths to control themselves than is required for the average person. This isn't surprising as it is very common for sociopaths to display impulsive traits.

Note: If you are particularly sensitive you may find the next section disturbing

Dysfunction in the Conscience Subsystem

History shows us time and time again that ordinary people are capable of shockingly vicious acts against other human beings. Whether we are referring to the Hutus suddenly murdering their Tutsi neighbors during the Rwandan genocide or when ordinary American men devastated the village of Mai Lai during the Vietnam War, the most important lesson we can learn from history is that given the right circumstances and social approval common people will perform unspeakably inhumane acts.

The reality is tough to accept, but the ordinary people you see walking down the street, in the grocery store, in class, or at the beach are the same sorts of people who brutalized the city of Nanjing, China. What's even more disturbing is that this doesn't just apply to strangers, even people close to you are capable of morally repugnant acts. This includes your colleagues, your friends, the people you look up to, your family, your children, and yourself.

When we understand the stakes, conscience becomes immeasurably important. The natural reaction to the aforementioned events is to imagine the perpetrators lacking conscience, but often this isn't the case. If anything their conscience is sometimes overactive.

The reason why ordinary people commit heinous acts is that their moral code has been infected by wicked beliefs about other human beings, and in some cases, their entire ethical system has been replaced by an evil ideology.

In order to be a good person, you not only need a powerful conscience, but you also need a resilient moral code which is capable of resisting the seduction of more degenerate beliefs in spite of career incentives, social pressures, and personal danger.

There are different ways to develop a resilient moral code; having a set of general principles guiding how you behave in the world is a time-tested approach to making ethical choices in tumultuous circumstances.

As mentioned earlier, your morality depends on a number of different factors including social pressures and life experiences. So the following intellectual exercise is limited in its ability to immediately change your actual behaviour. However, having a strong philosophical foundation will help you gradually improve your moral instincts and eventually give you the ability to resist participating in history's next great moral catastrophe.

> "Knowing your own darkness is the best method for dealing with the darkness of other people."
>
> Carl Jung

To prepare yourself for the possibility of being seduced into inhumane acts you first need to recognize the reality that you personally have the capacity to be an active participant in evil.

Many people hear about events where groups of ordinary citizens committed horrific crimes against humanity and imagine that they would be the one person who has the mental fortitude to say no. Statistically speaking, this is extremely unlikely. Perhaps you wouldn't be the most sadistic or enthusiastic participant, but chances are greater than not that you would be a reluctant collaborator at a minimum.

The best way to understand your own potential for evil is to study these historical events where gross atrocities were committed. Sympathizing with the victims is honourable and is a natural reaction for most people. But if you truly want to make progress in terms of knowing your own darkness you are better off empathizing with the perpetrators, i.e., appreciate their thinking and why they did what they did. Understand these events, particularly the minds of the perpetrators and you will be able to see the possibility for evil well before it actually occurs. By disturbing your own naivety, you will dramatically improve your capacity to say no, even when it is uncomfortable to do so. If you are unable to say no to small things, imagine how you will react when the stakes and social pressure is higher. Naivety is cute in a child, but a naive adult can become the pawn of evil.

> "My command is this: Love each other as I have loved you."
>
> John 15:12-13

Any love professed before accepting the evil within yourself is a love blinded by fear. Do you sincerely love or are you simply hiding the truth? Only when you have understood your own darkness are you truly strong and capable of genuine love.

However, accepting your darkness without love leads to cynicism. During the early 20th century Carl Panzram reportedly raped more than 1000 men and boys. Reading his memoirs, he makes it clear that he had not only accepted the darkness within himself, but he also worshipped it. Panzram never found love, in his own words, "I hate the whole damned human race, including myself".

By knowing your darkness you will develop tremendous strength, but what is the point of this strength if there is no love?

First love yourself, the higher-self is an untouchable flame inside of all of us which is the source of love for oneself and ultimately it is the reason why we should choose to live and not die. Your higher-self always loves you, and when you recognize this you can love yourself as well.

Once you love yourself, you can learn to love others. Love the victims, love the perpetrators, love everyone unconditionally. This the perfect ideal you will never reach, but you should always aim towards it.

"Every choice you make in your life should be made to increase your self-discipline."

Another impossible ideal which you should reach for. Discipline is the ultimate bulwark against anything which might threaten your righteousness.

In 1994 Josephine Dusaminama, a Hutu woman living in Kibuye Town in Rwanda risked everything. She saved a total 13 Tutsis by hiding them in her home and helping equip them to escape to the Congo which was known as Zaire at the time. Not only did she risk her life, but many other Hutu moderates were also tortured and raped. Her husband was strictly opposed to hiding Tutsis in the home and threatened to report her to the authorities if necessary to save himself.

The easiest, safest and most comfortable option would have been denying the Tutsis help or even becoming an active perpetrator in the genocide. Instead, Josephine Dusaminama displayed an unfathomable courage and self-discipline which was only matched by the evil of the offenders. She chose to live according to principles rather than submitting to her comfort. Josephine Dusaminama experienced fear and social pressure just like everyone else, but she had the discipline to act in spite of her fear, and that is what makes her a hero.

SELF-DISCIPLINE: THE ART OF BECOMING MORE HUMAN

Pauline Nyiramasuko was born in 1946 in Ndora, a small farming town in Rwanda. Her parents were poor, but she eventually proved herself extremely capable through her rapid rise in the Rwandan government. After finishing college, she moved to the capital city of Kigali and took up a job with the Ministry of Social Affairs. At 22 years of age, she was already a national inspector at the Ministry. Soon she married former speaker of parliament Maurice Ntahobari with whom she ended up having four children. In 1986 Pauline Nyiramasuko attended the National University of Rwanda to study law. And by 1992 she was the Minister for Family Welfare and the Advancement of Women in Rwanda. A very impressive career trajectory for the poor girl from the farming town of Ndora.

On April 25th, 1994, 19 days after the assasination of president Juvénal Habyarimanam, thousands of Tutsi were clustered together at a stadium where the Red Cross was providing food and shelter. That night, Pauline Nyiramasuko, her 24-year-old son Arsène Shalom Ntahobali, and a paramilitary group called Interahamwe surrounded the stadium. Under the command of Pauline Nyiramasuko and her son, the Interahamwe militia raped, tortured and killed the Tutsis seeking refuge with the Red Cross. In another event, Pauline Nyiramasuko ordered her men to burn a group of Tutsi women alive.

Pauline Nyiramasuko was sentenced to life imprisonment in 2011. She was the first woman ever to be convicted of genocide by an international court.

What explains the marked difference between these two women? Both coming from humble origins and both suffering pressures to conform. Was Pauline Nyiramasuko simply trying to protect herself and her family? After all numerous moderate Hutu politicians were murdered. Was she a sadist? Or did she simply hate the Tutsis so much that she felt like she needed to participate in their extermination? We can't know for certain what her motivations were, but we do know that seemingly well adjusted, and successful people like Pauline Nyiramasuko may, out of nowhere, display a terrible capacity for evil.

On the other hand, what made Josephine Dusaminama act differently? Her willingness to think for herself, her willingness to say no, and above all her courage. No one can expect to become as courageous as Josephine Dusaminama overnight. Instead, we can apply the three previous principles and relentlessly improve ourselves so we can become a human being who is willing and capable of resisting when it is necessary.

What is the difference between the Conscience and the Higher-Self?

The higher-self is an intelligence existing within our minds, which is the ideal manifestation of our current selves. It doesn't always know the truth, nor does it always know the best course of action. However, the higher-self's understanding is always the best which we are able to achieve at that particular moment, given our knowledge and mental resources.

The conscience, on the other hand, is much more limited in its function. It is simply meant to police your behaviour and pressure you to follow your own moral code.

Another major difference between these two subsystems is their primary objective. The main goal of the conscience is to have you act in a way which is ethical in relation to the collective groups you are a part of. The higher-self, on the other hand, is more focused on your progress as an individual. The higher-self certainly wants you to act morally, but it is more concerned with your self-interest than anything else.

Note: once you have developed substantially as an individual and you are secure in terms of finances, relationships, family, etc. Your higher-self might direct you to focus your energy on serving the greater society. This is because your higher-self understands that doing good for others, will for a lot of reasons, end up doing good for you as well.

These two programs are often in alignment. After all, the higher-self will usually advise you to listen to your conscience. The one case when they are not in alignment is when your higher-self is aware that your moral code has been corrupted. In this case, if you are able to communicate with your higher-self, it will advise you to go through the painful journey of discovering a new moral code.

THE IDENTITY

Our identity, commonly referred to as the ego by psychologists, is our sense of who we are and how we relate to the world. The subjective perception is that this sense of who we are is something deeply wired into us; this perception is an illusion. The reality is that our identity is actually very malleable, and we are capable of taking on a number of different roles within the greater society.

So why does our identity feel so stable and immovable? Identity hates change. It knows how common change is and does whatever it can, within its own power, to stay the same. Identity lies to us and tells us that not only is it unchangeable, but also that we can't act in a way which is contrary to our identity. The truth is that we can act despite our identity; we don't even necessarily need to change our identity first.

One of the reasons why identity is so successful in creating its fundamental illusion is that it has an alliance with the dopaminergic pathway mentioned earlier. When you try to change your identity or even simply act in opposition to your identity it uses the dopamine-reward pathway to punish you. On the other hand, if you act in line with your identity it rewards you. This is another reason why it is critical to become disciplined. You need to detach from negative and positive feelings if you want to be independent of your identity's control.

Changing your identity is simple, but that doesn't mean it is easy. Start acting as the person that you want to be, no matter how uncomfortable that feels. At first, your identity will do whatever it can to keep you the same, to prevent you from becoming the person your higher-self knows you ought to be. But, the identity is like a bully; it will back off after you put up enough resistance. Eventually, over time, your identity forms into something consistent with how you are acting.

To help illustrate all this very abstract discussion here is an example.

Let's say you have been a couch-potato for more than a decade. As a result, this has become a part of your identity. Your self-perception is that you are a person who doesn't enjoy exercise and avoids moving as much as possible.

You decide you don't like this identity and want to make exercise a regular part of your life, so you start going to the gym. Your identity fights back and makes the experience of exercising unbelievably uncomfortable. If your identity is clever it will wait a few weeks for your motivation to fizzle out. When your identity attacks, going to the gym is a massive chore. This is the testing point; if you give up now, your identity will become even stronger. Keep showing up to the gym according to your schedule no matter what.

Depending on the strength of your identity, it might take a while for it to give up, but after a couple of months of miserable defense against your identity's attacks eventually, it will realize that you have won the war. At this point your identity changes into something new; it decides that you are a fit person who enjoys going to the gym. The longer you keep up this habit, the more it will become an ingrained aspect of your identity.

The identity is not your enemy. Instead, it should be recognized for what it is, a force which attempts to keep your actions within a particular limited framework. In many situations, this is a very important and useful quality.

While it is possible to trudge forward using willpower alone, this can be like working against the current. If your identity is in agreement with your willpower, you will move towards your goals much more seamlessly. Your identity doesn't want to stop you from reaching your goals, it simply doesn't like to change. One option is to change your identity every time you have a new goal. This means tolerating weeks or even months of frustration as you and your identity go to battle until you win (presumably) and then have a cooperative identity up until the point when you need to change goals again.

An example would be a weightlifter who decides that they want to start running marathons. Not only is this a massive physical shift, but it is also an identity shift. After the first couple of weeks of motivation, his identity will start to protest his new diet and training regimen. It will use whatever mental tricks it has available to get him to return to his old patterns.

There is a better option. The ideal identity is one which doesn't need to change. Instead of attaching itself to a particular goal, ability and/or social group, this superior identity associates with discipline itself.

The ideal identity sees itself as someone who finds challenging or uncomfortable situations and pushes through to the goal despite feeling negative sensations. In the earlier example, the identity would not protest during the transition from weightlifter to long-distance runner; instead it would embrace the change as a new challenge.

It's unclear whether it is actually possible to achieve this perfect identity, likely you will always identify with something transient or mundane. However, just because an ideal can't be achieved, doesn't mean that you shouldn't move in the direction of that ideal.

SUBPERSONALITIES

Human beings have a number of subpersonalities which they can embody depending on the environment that they are in. Each of us has a different set of subpersonalities which change throughout the course of our lives. However, certain subpersonalities are found in many people, these include: a subpersonality for business environments, one for social situations, one for debates, a contemplative personality for thinking about an idea, and a subpersonality for brief interactions. Having a number of different subpersonalities is not a form of inauthenticity, they are after all legitimate aspects of the person.

There is a substantial minority of people who act in a similar way in every environment they are in. These people are not more authentic because of their indiscriminate behaviour, rather they are failing to adapt to social cues. Having a distinct set of subpersonalities is not something to be ashamed of, but rather something to harness and develop. Having the right subpersonality for a particular context will not only improve your effectiveness in that context but will also improve your ability to overcome discomfort in that kind of environment, i.e. improve your discipline.

Consider the different environments you are in on a regular basis. Do you have an appropriate subpersonality to match each of these contexts? For example, do you have a subpersonality which works well in business settings? Or do you have one you can use in social settings? If the answer is no to any of these questions, you ought to start the long process of cultivating a new subpersonality. The practical benefits are worth it, and you will grow in the process.

Most people don't develop their subpersonalities consciously; rather their subpersonalities emerge as a result of normal interactions. Nonetheless, it is likely that you didn't encounter the right environments to develop certain subpersonalities or you simply don't have a temperament which lends itself to a particular sort of subpersonality.

Developing a new or underdeveloped subpersonality involves three tasks.

1) Enter into the right setting for that subpersonality on a regular basis. If you want to develop your formal business subpersonality you ought to spend a lot of time in offices or other formal business environments.

2) Have the courage/vulnerability to actively engage with the new setting. If you want to develop your debating subpersonality you not only need to show up to join the group of friends who discuss contentious topics, but you also need to participate.

3) Reflect on the interactions you had, and try to understand how people were perceiving you, be honest with yourself.

If you have a subpersonality which is causing problems in your life, this likely speaks to a deeper problem which are the contexts that created and developed this subpersonality. For example, someone might have an extreme partying subpersonality who encourages them to drink in excess and makes bad decisions. The source of the problem is the amount and type of parties that the person attends. The way to eliminate a subpersonality is to simply avoid the environments which reinforce this personality. If the subpersonality has been operating for years or decades, it will take longer to eliminate.

Back to the partying example, if they stop attending the sorts of parties which activate the negative subpersonality it will gradually lose its influence over time. But, even if they don't go to the sorts of environments which activate the partying subpersonality, it can still be triggered by other cues such as seeing advertisements for a new club in town or being invited to a party by a friend.

The more the subpersonality is entrenched in your mind, the more convincing it will be. However, the more resilient the person is in avoiding the kinds of environments which release the negative subpersonality, the weaker and less influential it will become. Eventually, the subpersonality will be eliminated entirely.

What is the Difference Between the Identity and the Subpersonalities?

The identity is a general surface-level concept of who you are. On the other hand, a subpersonality is a series of behaviours, feelings, and cognitive operations which appear in certain environments. The identity is present in every single environment, while subpersonalities are triggered by certain cues.

Simulations of Other People

Amongst your many subsystems are simulations of other people, including family, friends, or colleagues whom you interact with regularly or people whose writing, movies, or social media you consume. Additionally, you likely have simulations based on people from your past, including teachers, counsellors, or childhood best friends living in your brain.

Simulations of other people may or may not be an accurate representation of the person, and the representation may continue to influence you well after that person has left your life (or has even died). This is why people go to see psychotherapists to deal with issues relating to their parents or past relationships. They likely have a cartoonish representation of someone who is negatively impacting their thoughts and behaviour.

Simulations can be very useful in your team of subsystems. Learn which simulation is most effective in particular kinds of situations. Bear in mind that in general your simulations are likely to be very inaccurate, except maybe with those simulations based on the people closest to you. And even with the people you know best, your simulations are probably a little off-base as well. While inaccurate simulations cause all kinds of relationship problems, that is outside the scope of this book.

In the context of discipline, inaccurate simulations may still be useful when they are effective. For example, many people have a cartoonish representation of certain historical figures; however, these incorrect simulations still inspire them to virtuous action. On the other hand, some of your inaccurate representations are likely to be influencing you negatively. You don't necessarily know which representations are accurate, so just don't allow any maladaptive representations to influence you.

There is an expression "You are the average of the five people you spend the most time with." This applies, at least in part, to your self-discipline as well, but it goes much further than just those five people. In fact, discipline is contagious, and all the people who are close to you will impact your discipline to some extent. The deeper the connection, the more impact they will have on your discipline. Anyone you interact with can potentially create a simulation in your mind, and the people who are closest to you are likely to have very impactful simulations.

Does that mean you are completely dependent on the discipline of the people around you? Not at all, it is absolutely possible to remain disciplined when everyone you interact with on a regular basis is lazy, weak, or undisciplined. It's just more challenging.

To optimize your discipline, you should work to surround yourself with the most disciplined people that you possibly can; this way, you will have more simulations influencing you to act in a more disciplined way.

But, if for whatever reason you are surrounded by undisciplined people don't use that as an excuse. It is always possible to dig deep and find discipline within yourself. There is no acceptable excuse for being undisciplined; this includes an undisciplined family, friend group, or undisciplined subsystems in your mind.

The Effect your Discipline has on other People

The contagious nature of discipline has an interesting implication. It means that if you change, the people around you will change as well. This should give you an additional motivation to become more disciplined. When you are disciplined, that rubs off on your friends, family, and even other people who barely know you, but when you are undisciplined people around you will be impacted in a negative way. Become a positive simulation for the people you influence.

You can actually use this fact for an awesome motivational effect; the following technique can refuel seemingly empty discipline storage. When you are tired or concerned that your discipline might give in focus on other people. If you are the leader of a team, understand that if you show weakness, your team will be more likely to give in. If you have people, who rely on you somehow make your performance about their success rather than your own. This technique is why, formerly undisciplined people are suddenly able to hold down a job after having kids. It is also why ordinary people in war are able to perform unimaginably brave and selfless acts.

Self-centered people are unable to find motivation in others and as a result, often struggle with discipline. It's no coincidence that the Hare Psychopathy Checklist includes both low empathy and high impulsivity. In the heat of the moment, think of how your actions will impact someone else and watch your discipline skyrocket.

Having simulations of other people in your mind is an inevitable part of being a human being who interacts with other human beings. It's not a bad or a good thing. What matters most is how you interact with the simulations in your mind and how you let them influence you.

Archetype Simulations

An archetype simulation is a subsystem with the qualities of a human being which represents a number of different individuals. Rather than creating a brand new simulation for every single person you meet, it is easier and more convenient to add them to an already well-developed archetype simulation.

This is the origin of stereotypes. A series of positive, negative, or neutral experiences with people from a certain group develops into an archetype simulation over time. Additionally, these group-simulations are informed by other influences, such as intellectuals, the media, the opinions of other people, and religion.

Archetype simulations can also form or can materialize from an innate and latent part of our minds. At birth, we already have the mental structures to develop certain archetype simulations; we simply require the necessary experiences for these archetype simulations to manifest themselves.

There are two main dangers associated with archetype simulations. The first is that just like regular simulations, they can be inaccurate. Secondly, even if the group-simulation is in fact accurate, the individual doesn't necessarily represent their group, and it is also very easy to assume an individual belongs to a group when in reality they have nothing to do with this particular group.

This all might seem very theoretical, so here are some practical examples.

1) A child has a negative relationship with a parent of either gender and as an adult ends up with a negative perception of masculinity or femininity as a whole.

2) An individual is taught certain things about people who pursue wealth and ends up grouping any business-minded person into the same category.

3) An individual has a series of similar experiences with intellectuals and categorizes any theoretically-minded or philosophically-minded person into the same group.

4) Someone has a couple of negative experiences with blue-collar workers and places every future blue-collared worker they meet into this negative category.

5) A child has a number of excellent experiences with different teachers, and as a result, when they are an adult, they end up associating teachers with certain positive qualities.

6) An individual has learned to associate aggressive posturing and loud yelling with dangerous people.

Is it desirable or even possible to completely eliminate group-simulations from our mind? The answer to both questions is no. In general, people within groups do tend to share some common traits on average, and it would impede our thinking to completely neglect this fact. However, the individual simulation is always more important than the group-simulation. Any individual is capable of transcending any group in which they belong.

You are your Discipline

People have a number of different perspectives as to what is meant by an individual, i.e. What is you and what is not you? Are you your entire body? Are you just your brain? Are you only an observer with no free will? And does this observer have a nonphysical spirit?

The truth is that you are your discipline. You are the force which can transcend the physical laws that normally govern the rest of your body and brain. Yes, much of your brain is outside of your control, that's why self-discipline isn't always easy. You are navigating a rowboat in the middle of a great ocean. Sometimes the currents are in your favor, sometimes they aren't, and sometimes terrible storms take over and leave you at the mercy of chaos.

Discipline is the art of becoming more conscious, transforming your rowboat into a dreadnought. Your subsystems are your crew, and they won't obey you mindlessly, after all, your subsystems have minds of their own. You have to care for them and understand their wants and desires, only then will they follow your lead.

When you recognize that you are the deciding force inside of your mind, it is easy to see the importance of becoming more disciplined. In the pursuit of improving your discipline, you grow the essential aspects of yourself.

Seeing yourself as your discipline can be a tough pill to swallow, especially if your discipline is weak. Many people abandoned their self-discipline at a young age in favor of hedonic pleasures; these people abandoned themselves.

The ironic fact is that the deepest pleasures can only be experienced through the strongest and most resilient expressions of discipline.

Those who abandoned themselves a long time ago should not feel hopeless. We are fortunate in that discipline can survive any beating. No matter how long it has been dormant, discipline can achieve its rightful place as the leading subsystem of the mind.

4. Creating an Effective Team of Subsystems

Your subsystems work together much like the employees in a company. When the right people are in the right positions, and when everyone is working towards the same goal, the company operates more efficiently. However, if there are internal conflicts or people aren't working in the best job for their particular skill set, the company itself will suffer.

Just like a real company, your subsystems will never entirely get along, and occasionally some of your subsystems will work in their own interest instead of your greater interest. While you will likely never achieve perfection, you still want your subsystems to operate in the most effective way possible.

The first step is to reorganize the power structure amongst your subsystems.

Discipline (you), should be the CEO of your mind. Discipline can and should consult the other subsystems in making its decisions, but in an effective company, discipline makes the final decision.

Your **higher-self** doesn't want to be in charge, but it ought to be the closest advisor to your discipline. The identity will aggressively try to take this close advisor role, but it is critical to make sure that the higher-self holds the position. The higher-self won't fight for power, you need to recognize its competence and keep listening to its suggestions.

The **dopamine reward pathway, the risk assessment system and the identity** should be relegated to less influential positions where they are consulted for their opinion only at times when it is appropriate. These subsystems are like aggressive employees who think that they deserve executive positions when in reality, they are not to be trusted with major responsibilities. However, they all have useful functions and should be allowed to operate in the right situation.

Ideally, **motivation** is influential when it is on a high and not influential when it is on a low. But, unlike the other subsystems, it's often impossible to choose motivation's influence. A better long-term strategy is to acquire enough discipline to temper motivation when it is on a low.

Oftentimes, the best executive subsystems are the **simulations of other people** that you have in your mind. This includes people you know personally as well as people who you have never met, but who's content (books, podcasts, videos, etc.) you consume.

The executive positions can have specific functions, for example, you might draw upon one person when making relationship decisions, and you might draw upon another person when making financial decisions. Alternatively, executive positions don't have to have a specific function; instead they can perform more general duties.

Another great executive is your **simulation of you in the future**. This can be you in 5 years, 20 years, or even 40 years. This subsystem is so useful that it actually makes sense to use both the you 5 years into the future and the you 20 years in the future depending on the specific situation.

It is critical to choose executive subsystems who want the best for you. Consider whether or not the people who influence you are interested in your success or if they have other motivations such as boosting their own ego. Don't worry if you promote the wrong person to an executive role; with some effort you can always rearrange your c-suite later.

So long as your moral code hasn't been corrupted, your conscience should be on your executive team. With all the power you gain in accruing discipline, you ought to have a moral force directing that energy.

A well developed, emotionally intelligent **subpersonality** is a great addition to the executive team. In fact, many of your subpersonalities can eventually reach a point where they are worthy of executive status. On the other hand, a new or for whatever reason, underdeveloped subpersonality can be cartoonish and based on an exaggerated understanding of some particular environment. Additionally, an immature subpersonality might believe that whatever it does is the most important aspect of your life and pressure you to move in that direction constantly.

For example, your debating subpersonality may value establishing truth or winning an argument above all else. This can cause a lot of problems in social and business environments. A good approach would be to have a conversation with your debating subpersonality and explain why winning an argument is often not the best way to win at life.

Finally, certain simulations based on real people are negative influences. They ought to be demoted or even fired depending on the situation. There are countless ways in which people influence you negatively, whether you know them personally or not. Don't be afraid to take these subsystems out of commission.

Finding Better External Subsystems

Many people understand the importance of having strong role models, and they can also see the downside of having poor role models. Despite this, very few people intentionally evaluate the role models they already have or seek out new superior role models.

There are a few different reasons for this.

1) Some people see themselves as an autonomous entity who isn't influenced by other people, so finding a role model seems unnecessary. They may see role models as being useful for people in general, but they don't apply this to themselves.

2) The idea of having a role model is damaging to some people's identity because it implies inferiority to someone else. Even if this were true, it would be a poor reason to avoid role models; however, it's actually inaccurate. You don't have to be inferior to someone else to benefit from their insights, and having a simulation of them in your mind can be very useful. In fact, you and your role models can even learn from each other.

3) Some people think that they are too old to search for a role model. The truth is that as you get older, you acquire more wisdom and as a result, are better at assessing which role models would be

beneficial for you and which would influence you in a negative way. It's well known that young people are often damaged by the impact of poor role models in their lives; this is less likely to be a problem for older people.

4) Some people simply haven't even considered the idea of finding new role models.

A role model is essentially a simulation of another person which has a lot of influence in your mind. When it comes to finding new subsystems, you can either seek out people in person and try to develop a relationship with them or you can find people who produce consumable content and add them to your executive subsystems.

Face-to-face Influences

The people who you regularly interact with face-to-face will more easily become influential subsystems in your mind. Normally, a number of your executive subsystems are already simulations of people you know personally.

For some people, it is difficult to find beneficial role models amongst the people they currently know. Not everyone is blessed to be in a community of happy, well-adjusted, disciplined people. The good news is that you only need two or three role models whom you know in person. Even one strong role model can make a big difference.

Don't rush the process. Vet anyone whom you are considering adding to your executive team. Get to know them well and watch how they behave in different situations. Are they contemplative and emotionally intelligent? Or are they ego-drive and rash in their judgments?

CONTENT CREATORS

The term "Content Creator" has become an overused buzzword normally associated with social media. However, it can refer to anyone who makes some kind of consumable informational product. This includes writers, podcasters, and video creators.

There are countless people producing content who could potentially be a positive influence. Accessing this content is easier than ever with the various media sharing platforms and the internet in general.

The advantage of using content creators as executive subsystems is that you have more options and as a result, are able to choose the perfect influence for you personally. Additionally, you have access to some of the wisest and most disciplined people in the world.

Another advantage of using content creators as executive subsystems is that unlike people who you know face-to-face if a content creator becomes a poor influence, you can drop them from your life immediately. In fact, this is the recommended approach. Keep content creators as executive subsystems as long as they are useful when your life changes direction or the content creator changes their style simply find someone new.

In the same way that you would vet people you know in person, you should also vet content creators before making them executive subsystems in your mind. With content creators, you can and ought to be much choosier. Not only do you have access to some of the best influences in the world, but you also have access to some of the worst.

Here is a list of things to look out for when choosing content creators as executive subsystems.

1) They should be extremely disciplined in their own lives. When you make a subsystem influential in your mind, the traits of that person will start to rub off on you in unexpected ways. Even if you chose them for a different reason, their discipline (or lack thereof) will reflect on you.

2) They should have a well-developed conscience. Many influential content creators aren't interested in improving the lives of their audience; instead they are mostly trying to grow their audience and/or earn as much money as they can. There is nothing wrong with an ambitious content creator or a content creator who charges money; the problem is when they aren't actually trying to make their audience's lives better. For example, a content creator who creates controversial material for the sole purpose of gaining attention online is not a good influence. It is better to use content creators who rely on the quality of their material to build their audience.

3) They should be introspective, self-aware, and open-minded. There are some content creators who genuinely want the best for their audience, but have a very narrow view of what people ought to be doing with their lives.

4) They should regularly discuss and advocate the changes you want to make in your life. If you want to improve your business, find a small business podcast. If you want to improve your physical condition, find a good fitness-themed channel on youtube. Their

influence will increase your motivation and will give you all kinds of useful information as well.

The potential disadvantage of using content creators as executive subsystems is that compared to people you know face-to-face, it can be more difficult for their subsystems to reach a long-term influential status in your mind. If you stop consuming a content creator's material, it won't take long for them to lose influence in your mind. However, this is arguably not a disadvantage.

The suggestion in this book is that subsystems of people you know in person should be thought of in terms of their impact over the course of years or decades, while content creators should be used more often for their immediate benefit.

Once you have decided that a particular content creator will be a beneficial addition to your list of executive subsystems, start consuming their content on a daily basis and thinking about their ideas regularly as well. It shouldn't take long for them to start influencing your thoughts and daily decisions.

Can you change the Nature of Subsystems based on other People?

Some people might read this chapter and wonder if they can take an existing subsystem based on another person and improve it. For example, a particular subsystem is benefitting you substantially in certain ways, but you want to make the subsystem more disciplined.

The answer is that this isn't a fruitful strategy. You can try to change aspects of their character, but any time you see this person in real life, see them on social media, or consume their content you will be reminded of the real version of them. You can try to block out these reminders, but unfortunately, the mind doesn't work like that. Your best bet would be to find a new subsystem to replace them or to simply deal with the subsystem's deficit.

The exception to this rule are subsystems based on religious or ancient historical figures. Much of the facts relating to the distant past are hotly debated by historians and other scholars so there are a lot of reasonable perspectives on well-known people from the past. If you have any religious or any historical figures among your executive subsystems, it is best to interpret them in the way which seems right to you.

Unification of your Subsystems

Just as important as assigning roles for your subsystems is making sure that your subsystems are working together. In fact, the unification of your subsystems is a fundamental aspect of developing self-discipline.

If you (your discipline) create a goal and then another subsystem (or a team of subsystems) temporarily gains influence and attempts to sabotage your efforts, you may not achieve your goal. This is a failure of discipline.

Even if you are able to suppress a specific subsystem and prevent it from influencing you, your discipline will be partially drained. The sheer act of ignoring or suppressing a subsystem requires effort, and this effort would be better served doing other things.

This is why unifying your subsystems or at least creating order within your subsystems is necessary to become the most disciplined version of yourself.

As mentioned earlier, it is impossible for your subsystems to always get along, that being said, there is a huge difference between a company where the subsystems are mostly on the same page and a company where the subsystems are in constant conflict.

If your subsystems have been assigned the correct roles, it will be easier for you to create unification. Since your executive subsystems want the best for you and are presumably reasonable and rational, their common goals make it simpler for them to get along.

Certain subsystems will predictably work against the other subsystems in particular situations. For example, the identity and the dopamine reward pathway will team up to try to sabotage any efforts you make to change company direction.

Since you know this is going to happen go ahead and preemptively demote both of these programs before making any major changes to your behaviour. Do this by detaching yourself from positive and negative emotions.

As mentioned previously, the identity uses the dopamine reward pathway to limit rewards whenever you act in a way contrary to your current identity, and it rewards you whenever you act in accordance with your current identity.

By detaching yourself from positive and negative emotions, your identity and its partner, the dopamine reward pathway lose their control over you. You are free to act in accordance with your goal of changing direction.

If, on the other hand, your aim is to continue in a way which is consistent with your current identity, feel free to allow your identity and the dopamine reward pathway to influence you. Your identity can be a powerful force when it is unified with your greater aims.

The **risk assessment system** is capable of unifying with your overall company objectives. However, this may take some time. It is a slow system to adapt, but once it understands what you want and what you want to avoid, it can be a very useful tool for you and your executive subsystems. In order to get your risk assessment system onboard, you will first need to follow the instructions given earlier on how to improve its function. Once it is operating effectively for the modern world, it can start to actually be useful. Next, rather than have your risk assessment system control your behaviour, have it send you signals which indicate the danger potential in different situations. This way, you can balance risk with benefit and make a rational decision.

Conscience will unify with the other subsystems if the most influential subsystems in your mind are in accordance with your moral code. Normally there will be some disagreement as to the most moral actions among your executive subsystems; however, if your moral code is good and your executive program have been chosen well, there shouldn't be any massive paralyzing disagreements.

Unifying **motivation** with the other subsystems is tricky because it seems to follow up and down cycles mostly independent of whatever else you do. That being said there are some things you can do to have motivation work together with the other subsystems as much as possible. When your motivation is high, this is a great time to get a lot of work done or do things which would normally be uncomfortable for you. On the other hand, when your motivation is low, you should aim to maintain all of your basic goals and obligations.

Occasionally your motivation will be low, but you simply won't have the luxury of taking things easy. Life obligations will require a larger than normal output. In this case, the best way to unify your programs while meeting general life requirements is to apply some of the motivation triggers mentioned earlier. However, do your best to avoid situations where you need to rely on motivational triggers because they don't always work.

In order to unify your **subpersonalities** with your other subsystems, it is important to recognize that immature subpersonalities have fairly self-evident agendas. An immature formal business subpersonality wants you to earn money and succeed at your career above all else. An immature social subpersonality values your time with your friends more than anything else.

An immature subpersonality trying to push you in a specific direction can be ignored; however the energy needed to ignore their influence can be taxing. The solution is to help that subpersonality mature. You do this by explaining to them the vital importance of the other aspects of your life. For example, you could explain to an immature social subpersonality that friends alone won't give you security or a sense of meaning in your life. While strong friendships are important for your happiness, other aspects of your life, such as career, learning, and family, are critical as well.

SELF-DISCIPLINE: THE ART OF BECOMING MORE HUMAN

It is impossible to completely unify all the different "other people simulations" and "future self simulations" that you have in your mind. That being said, the team of executives you chose earlier should be unified under the single goal of improving your discipline and making your life better.

If one of your executive subsystems is opposed to a decision you make, start up a dialogue with this subsystem. Try to understand its position and then explain to your subsystem why you are making the choice that you are making. Just like a real human in a real organization, you ought to treat your subsystems with respect and help them understand the direction you are going in.

The following is an example which illustrates the fairly odd recommendation above. Let's say you are entering into the legal profession and are deciding on which area of law you want to pursue. Based on your skillset, interests, and connections, you have two main options.

Corporate Law: Much higher salary, but higher stress levels and longer working hours.

Human Rights Law: Lower salary, but very meaningful to you personally.

You and the majority of your executive subsystems decide that Human Rights Law, despite the lower salary, is actually the better option for you personally. However, one of your executive subsystems is based on your very intelligent and successful aunt who values earning money above all else.

Instead of demoting this subsystem, after all, money is important, and your aunt does have a lot of great insights, you should try to explain to her your motivations. Literally have a conversation with this subsystem in your mind. You could explain that ever since you were in high school, you always wanted to protect the rights of innocent people. Also, you could explain how you aren't interested or capable of meeting the time and stress demands of corporate law. If your aunt is a reasonable person then the simulation of her in your mind should be reasonable as well. By explaining your choice, your aunt subsystem will be in agreement with you, and your subsystems will be unified on this issue.

When you are trying to unify your subsystems, there will be some subsystems based on other people who aren't in an official executive role, but are still able to gain influence. In some cases, these "other people subsystems" will work in alignment with the executive team, but in other cases, they will try to influence you in a different direction.

It is impossible and not necessarily desirable to eliminate all of these influential subsystems based on other people who didn't make the executive cut. After all, the huge variety of simulations in your mind is part of what makes your thinking nuanced. That being said, it is certainly beneficial to recognize the existence of these subsystems and understand when they will contribute to your goals and when they will interfere.

For example, you might have a friend or a family member who wants the best for you and whose subsystem is useful to you in certain circumstances. However, they have some fundamental flaws in their value system or thinking process, which means that they can't be given an executive position in your mind. This subsystem should still be allowed to exist in your mind, and you shouldn't try to eliminate it, that being said, the more you understand it, the more beneficial and the less harmful it will be.

Likely you have subsystems based on people who legitimately want the best for you, but who's negative qualities significantly outnumber their positive qualities. From the perspective of optimizing your subsystems, you would want to stop associating with this person, however, often social obligations or your desire to be fair to this person prevent you from breaking the connection.

The good news is that it is possible to interact with someone on a regular basis, but not allow their subsystem to hold an influential place in your mind. In fact, this is straightforward if you recognize the person as being a poor influence as soon as you meet them. The challenge is when their subsystem has already built up an influential position in your mind.

For example, a parent who wants the best for you, but who is at the same time severely lacking in emotional intelligence. Another example is a close friend who truly cares about you, however, despite being in their mid-thirties has yet to take on the life perspective of an adult.

The correct course of action is to continue interacting with this person, but to avoid discussing your deepest values or important life decisions with them. Keep the conversations light or discuss subjects removed from your life. Good conversation topics include sports, history, television, and novels. Bad conversation topics include philosophy, career goals, romantic relationships, or children.

If you continue to interact with them on a regular basis their subsystem will continue to influence you in subtle ways. However, if you recognize that they are a poor influence and at the same time avoid more serious conversation topics, their subsystem will lose most of its ability to affect your mind.

You may have subsystems based on friends, family members, associates, or celebrities who don't want the best for you at all. If this is the case, whenever possible, stop thinking about and stop interacting with that person in real life. Stop following them on social media and avoid them as much as possible in social gatherings.

The problem is that some of the time, you won't be able to avoid interacting with people like this. For example, a vindictive colleague who you work with every single day. Or a close family member who resents your success.

The first thing to do is to attempt to disarm this person by improving your relationship with them; however, the specific techniques needed to do this are extremely complex, situation-specific and beyond the scope of this book. We are going to assume that you pursued every effort to optimize your relationship with this person, and for whatever reason, your efforts failed.

In this extreme scenario where your attempts to improve the relationship failed, but at the same time you need to interact with this person, the first thing to do is to recognize that their subsystem will continue to exist in your mind. The natural reaction will be to fight against this subsystem and prevent it from influencing you at all. This is the correct approach; however, you don't want to fight against their subsystem too aggressively because there can be a serious negative side effect. You may feel inclined to do the opposite of what they want. For example, let's say that you have a jealous parent who despises your intelligence or some other positive quality that you have. At the same time, they are trying to pressure you to study engineering. Perhaps you have no interest in engineering and don't have any special talent for the field. You are likely to become frustrated by your parent's pressure and myopic perspective. Many people in this situation rebel by doing the opposite of what their parent would want instead of actually making the best decision for themselves.

Maybe if you studied medicine, you would have a stable, fulfilling long-term career which matches your skills and interests. You would be able to see this life path clearly if you weren't blinded by your parent's subsystem. Instead, you end up rebelling by joining a commune and cutting off connection with your entire family for five years. The correct strategy is subtle. Don't let their subsystem influence you directly, but at the same time, don't fight against it too aggressively. Transcend its influence by smiling or laughing when it starts speaking in your mind.

Finally, when you encounter dark or evil people don't be afraid to keep their subsystems around. You want to prevent them from influencing your behaviour as much as possible; however, they can give you insight into the way morally corrupt people think. This will give you a better understanding of your own darkness as well as prevent you from being taken advantage of by other unscrupulous people.

How to Eliminate a Subsystem

Oftentimes, we have one or a number of different subsystems which do more harm than good. In this case, we want to demote and ideally eliminate this maladaptive subsystem.

The longer a subsystem has existed, the more influence it has been able to acquire and therefore, the more difficult it will be to eliminate. Additionally, subsystems have minds of their own and survival instincts, which make them more resilient and more effective at thwarting your efforts to get rid of them.

There are two main ways to eliminate a maladaptive subsystem. For certain subsystems, both of the following techniques will work, for other subsystems, only one of the two techniques will work. We will be analyzing these techniques separately.

The first technique involves simply preventing the subsystem from operating. This is the technique which was recommended earlier for subpersonalities. Usually, subsystems will have a trigger or multiple triggers which set them off. This strategy for eliminating subsystems simply involves preventing that subsystem from being triggered.

As mentioned in the previous section, to apply this technique to a subsystem based on another human being simply stop interacting with the actual person. Mute them on social media and avoid them as much as possible.

The second technique for eliminating a subsystem involves allowing the subsystem to be triggered, but then immediately using your discipline to prevent it from executing its function.

This technique is very effective for eliminating cognitive or behavioural patterns.

For example, if you respond to heavy traffic with anger, intentionally put yourself into a traffic jam, but instead of responding with anger take deep breaths through your nose into your lower abdomen and think happy thoughts. Do this multiple times a week, and you will quickly find that your tendency to overreact to frustrating situations on the road is eliminated or reduced dramatically.

Certain subsystems cannot be eliminated entirely; they are simply too deeply entrenched into the structure of your mind and brain. These are motivation, the dopamine reward pathway, the risk assessment system, and the identity.

Fortunately, there is no reason to want to eliminate these programs entirely, but reducing their influence is possible and is often a good idea. Suggestions for mediating their influence can be found in each of their respective sections.

5. Self-Knowledge

Self-knowledge and self-discipline go hand in hand. Yes, it is possible to develop self-discipline without improving your self-knowledge and vice versa, but your whole journey will be much smoother if you are able to develop your self-knowledge as well.

Self-knowledge means knowing who you are without bias from ego or from your short-term feelings. This is surprisingly tricky. The challenge is to see yourself from a detached perspective. This means that your self-assessment doesn't depend on how you feel right now and isn't designed to satisfy what you want to believe about yourself.

Understanding yourself isn't something that you will have achieved at some point. Just like discipline, self-knowledge is a lifelong pursuit. And similar to discipline, there are different forms of self-knowledge. You might have a good understanding of your abilities and how other people perceive you, but you might not know what you want or what you ought to be doing.

Ultimately, the more self-knowledge you develop, the more effective you will be.

Commit to your Goals

From now on, barring some kind of extreme unforeseeable circumstance, you need to commit to completing every goal you set for yourself. You might say that your goal is to get a promotion, and that there is no way you can guarantee success. Or maybe your goal is to win your next martial arts tournament, but you can't guarantee that you will perform your best that day.

These are the wrong types of goals.

Effort based goals are better than performance goals. Instead of saying that you will get a promotion by this day next year, commit to showing up for work 30 minutes early and staying 30 minutes late every single day, that way you are entirely in control of whether or not you will succeed. Instead of making your goal winning the martial arts tournament commit to practicing 2 hours a day and cooking at home instead of eating fast food.

You shouldn't ever set a goal you won't achieve, this is lying to yourself, and it creates a pattern of not sticking with things. You want to develop confidence in your ability to maintain habits over the long-term.

It is very realistic for you to go to the gym every single day for the next 5 years, but very few people are able to sustain their habits for this long. The reason why is that they haven't developed patterns of sticking with their goals. Perhaps they set too many goals while in a motivated state or maybe their goals are too performance-based and they aren't always able to meet their expectations.

Even if right now you are struggling to stick with new habits for a month, if you follow the recommendations in this book, you will be able to stick to habits for years or even decades.

By maintaining habits for years at a time, you will develop a long-term knowledge unavailable to most people. How many people do you know who say that they are going to stick to some habit, but only last a couple of months or even less? This is because they lack in long-term knowledge, their behaviour depends more on the people around them and the influences of their environment than it does on their individual will.

In fact, most people who stick with things for a long time are only doing it because the people influencing them push them in that direction. For example, many people with low levels of discipline are able to show up for work every single day because of social pressures and a fear of getting fired. While it is very useful to take advantage of these kinds of external pressures, you also want to be able to maintain long-term habits entirely based on your own conscious will.

In the beginning, your self-knowledge might not be up to par. You may very well set some goals which are too much for your discipline to handle or maybe you set goals that are too easy. As you gain experience, you will learn how to set goals which challenge your self-discipline, but are still within reach if you put in your best effort.

Some people perform well when they have a very challenging goal which they aren't sure if they can reach. The good news is that if you respond well to this kind of challenge, there is an exception to the previous rule. This is when you create a distinction in your mind between stretch-goals and definite-goals.

A stretch-goal is something you are aiming for, but aren't sure if you can achieve it. On the other hand, a definite-goal is something you know that you can accomplish and will achieve no matter what.

If you do decide to use stretch-goals, you still need to make sure that you always follow through with your definite-goals. It is okay to underperform on a stretch-goal occasionally, but never fail to follow through with a definite-goal. Underperforming on a stretch-goal is not lying to yourself simply because you aren't making any commitments to actually achieving the goal.

Just so you never feel tempted to be dishonest with yourself, it makes sense to use a special word when you set a definite-goal. For example, you could say "absolutely" before every definite-goal. So if you say "I will try to run 15 kilometers today" that is a stretch goal, and you don't have to reach it. However, if you say "I will absolutely run 5 kilometers today" that is a definite-goal and you have no option but completing your 5 kilometers (barring injury or other extreme circumstances). Attaching special importance to a word like "absolutely" might seem silly, but it will give your discipline immense power.

Detachment Techniques to Develop Self-Knowledge

Detachment is the ability to temporarily disconnect from your identity and see your situation from the perspective of an unbiased observer. A very effective detachment technique is to ask one of your executive "other people subsystems" what they think about a particular situation. You want to assume that they know everything you know, even if this isn't realistic. This technique is great for disconnecting from what you want to believe and getting a more realistic understanding of the situation. You can use someone whom you know in person or someone whose content you consume regularly.

Another detachment technique, which is useful for disconnecting yourself from the whims of the moment, is to imagine your perspective in 5 years, 10 years, 20 years or some other amount of time. This particular technique is effective because it allows you to access your higher-self.

It is always possible to access and communicate with your higher-self. Over time as your relationship with your higher-self improves, you and your higher-self will be able to communicate more easily. Eventually, after working on your self-knowledge for years, you will merge with your higher-self and learn to detach effortlessly.

Writing to Improve Self-Knowledge

Writing improves your self-knowledge in part because it is a detachment technique. When you put your ideas down on paper, you are able to more easily see them from the perspective of someone else. This detachment effect is particularly pronounced when you look at your writing months, years, or even decades later.

Another reason why writing is beneficial is that it improves your long-term knowledge of yourself. In the future, you will forget the majority of the thoughts, ideas, and feelings that you are having right now. But if you have them written down, you will get a window into your past self.

Think back 5 years or to a time in the past when you weren't writing or recording your thoughts and feelings. How much do you remember about yourself? Chances are you are only able to recall some brief images, sensations, and feelings related to the time. Unless you have a special kind of memory, you likely don't have a detailed picture.

On the other hand, if you had been writing every single day, you would be able to look back and see exactly what you were up to at any given time. This means that you will have a clear, well-recorded history of the development of your own mind.

Writing also helps you gauge the quality of your ideas. If you never write your ideas down, it is easy to fool yourself into believing that your ideas are more clever or more original than they actually are.

When you write your ideas down and justify them in writing, you will get a more realistic sense of the logical foundations and clarity of your own thinking. In fact, by writing down your ideas, you hold your thinking to a higher standard and actually improve your logical ability.

So what kind of writing is optimal? Whichever kind you will actually do.

Journaling is great for people who normally don't enjoy writing because it helps them organize their thoughts without the pressure of having to present them to anyone else. A daily journaling habit is very beneficial, in fact, many people have actually converted their journal entries into complete essays and books.

Fiction doesn't work for everyone, but if it works for you, you will find some unique self-knowledge benefits from writing fiction. The characters in your stories will likely represent parts of yourself or the people in your life. By observing how the story unfolds, you will get a window into the workings of your own subconscious.

Writing non-fiction books articles, or essays is a great way to deepen your thinking and clarify your logical processes. It is a challenging form of discipline in itself because you need to consistently create content, but at the same time, your writing needs to be pertinent and accurate.

Pushing Yourself to the Limit

When you are sitting on a comfortable couch in a well-heated room in your house, it is easy to imagine yourself doing all kinds of incredible things. But to truly get a sense of your own abilities, how you respond in stressful situations, and how much resolve you actually have it is necessary to push your limits. This means going on a multi-day trek in the wilderness, competing in a powerlifting tournament, starting a new business or traveling to a part of the world you have never been to before. There is no limit to the number of different ways you can push yourself. What's important is that you attempt something where you don't know how you will respond or something which you don't know if you will be able to actually complete.

You might be wondering, isn't that contradictory to the idea that you should never set a goal you can't accomplish? It isn't, in this situation where you are pushing yourself to the limit you aren't actually setting a goal; instead you are testing yourself. When you do push yourself to the limit make sure to not see it as a definite-goal in your mind. Sure, you can make your goal to try your absolute best, but be indifferent to the outcome of your test.

Listen to Other People or Listen to Yourself?

Deciding whether or not you should listen to someone else can be tricky because many people have warped inaccurate perceptions of you and some other people don't even have your best interests at heart. Knowing who you can listen to and recognizing which topics they understand and which topics they don't understand is critical.

In the same way that you have simulations of other people, they also have subsystems based on you. When you listen to other people's perception of you, they are giving you the results of their simulation (assuming that they are being honest).

Certain people's simulations of you will be more accurate than others. This usually depends on how close the person is to you and how long they have known you. Overall, your closest friends and family will have the most accurate simulations.

Additionally, some people's subsystems will be more or less accurate in certain situations. This depends on what they have seen you do. For example, someone who has never seen you undergo hardship won't be able to accurately predict how you will react to a challenging situation.

It is very likely that you have been categorized, whether intentionally or unintentionally, into other people's archetype simulations. Archetype simulations were discussed in more detail in a previous chapter. As a quick reminder, this means that they are associating you with other people who belong to groups which you may or may not be a part of. If you are unlike the other people in the groups which they are associating you with, their perceptions of you can be very inaccurate.

When you are interacting with someone, it is important to understand how often they are putting you into a group-simulation and how often they are treating you as an individual. In some cases, you may actually conform to the group that they are associating you with, but much of the time these group-simulations will cloud their thinking.

Bearing in mind all of the different ways in which someone's perception of you can be inaccurate, it still sometimes makes sense to seek out the opinions of others. This is because there are a number of cognitive biases which can make it difficult to get a realistic understanding of yourself. Occasionally there are things which nearly everyone else can see but remain a blind spot for you. Two potential problems to be aware of are the self-serving bias and cognitive dissonance.

THE SELF-SERVING BIAS

This bias is a well-researched phenomenon in experimental psychology. In order to sustain a sense of self-esteem, people tend to interpret things in a way which bolsters their own feelings of self-worth. The self-serving bias can manifest itself in obvious ways, particularly with arrogant or narcissistic people. Additionally, the self-serving bias can also be more subtle. People tend to attribute their success to their abilities and efforts, while attributing their failures to external events.

Picture a runner who is able to complete one marathon and is unable to complete another. According to the self-serving bias, she is likely to attribute her success in the first marathon to her diligent preparation and natural aptitude for running. On the other hand, she is likely to attribute her failure in the second marathon to external factors such as bad weather or poor path markings.

The reason why this bias can be particularly subtle and difficult to sniff out is that the runner might be partially correct. Perhaps she truly does have a natural aptitude for running, a consistent training plan and in the run where she failed perhaps there truly was bad weather and poor path markings.

But, if she hadn't been influenced by the self-serving bias she might have attributed her success and failures to less self-serving factors. She could have blamed her failure in the second run to the fact that she didn't consume enough food the day before and she could have credited her success in the first run to the enthusiastic crowd cheering her on.

The truth is that in most situations attributing a single cause to your success or failure is incorrect. Most of the time, a number of different factors contribute to your performance. For a runner, this includes the elements listed in the previous paragraph as well as a whole host of other considerations.

Note: there are certain situations where a single event or factor has a disproportionate effect on whether you succeed or fail. For example, if the runner had stepped in a hole and sprained her ankle. But, these sorts of events are uncommon, most of the time there are a wide array of elements contributing to the eventual result.

The self-serving bias is the function of the identity; most people's identities hold flattering views of themselves. Even if your identity has some negative self-perceptions, at a fundamental level, it is likely to see itself in a positive light.

COGNITIVE DISSONANCE

Psychologist Leon Festinger originally published a paper on cognitive dissonance in 1957, the essential aspects of his theory have held up throughout decades of experimental research. According to the cognitive dissonance model, people will either change their behaviour or change their thinking in response to psychological discomfort, i.e. inconsistencies.

The best way to understand cognitive dissonance is through an example. The following is an outline of the first experiment done on cognitive dissonance in 1959. The researchers were actually Leon Festinger and his colleague Merrill Carlsmith. 71 Participants in the experiment were required to spend an hour performing a very boring task (moving spools of thread a quarter clockwise turn). Then the participants were randomly split into three groups.

Two of these groups were asked to convince another participant that the task isn't boring, but is actually fun to do. One of these groups was paid 1 dollar to do the convincing, and the other group was paid 20 dollars. The final group wasn't asked to convince anyone of anything.

Afterward, all three groups were asked how enjoyable they found the task of moving the spools of thread. As expected by the researchers, the participants who were paid 1 dollar to convince people that the task was fun rated the task as more enjoyable than the participants in the other two groups.

So how did the experimenters predict this result, and how does it relate to cognitive dissonance theory? In the 20 dollar condition, the participants were able to justify their actions by the external reward of 20 dollars. But, in the 1 dollar condition, the participants didn't have sufficient external justification for their actions.

They had just told someone that the task was fun for not much of a reward at all. In order to relieve the inconsistency in their thinking and behaviour they changed their thinking and convinced themselves that moving spools of thread was actually enjoyable and not a boring task.

There is an extensive body of research on cognitive dissonance (and some competing theories). It is beyond the scope of this book to investigate all of this research; however, you can rest assured that there are numerous other experiments confirming the same kinds of findings.

Cognitive dissonance isn't exactly a cognitive bias in the formal sense. But, the instinct to reduce cognitive dissonance can get in the way of clear thinking about oneself. Your self-knowledge will be severely impaired if you respond to mental discomfort by changing your beliefs.

For example, if you lie to other people often, but hold the belief that lying is wrong, cognitive dissonance theory suggests that there are three ways to respond to the inconsistency. First, you can change your belief that lying is wrong and come to accept yourself as a liar. Second, you can fix the inconsistency by actually believing your own lies.

Finally, you can change your behavior by breaking your negative habit of lying. In this situation, the best decision would be the third and final option; however, many people are less virtuous in their approach.

Bringing it together

So this is the tricky situation that you are in. Other people are wrong about you some of the time, and you are wrong about you some of the time as well. The trick is to know when you can trust yourself and if you can't trust yourself, know whom you can trust instead.

Listening to yourself requires getting in touch with your higher-self. Over time, through introspection, you will get better at knowing when you are communicating with your higher-self and when you are communicating with a different subsystem.

If you are in communication with your higher-self and it doesn't know the answer to a question, it will be honest and tell you. In this event, you can consult one of the other subsystems in your mind (you in the future, someone you respect), or you can actually consult another person whom you know well. The best person to ask is someone who has seen you in a similar situation and has the necessary expertise to make a rational assessment of the situation.

For example, a parent will likely know you well enough to help you decide if you should choose a career in medicine or a career in engineering, but they might not have the specific knowledge to help you decide between anesthesiology and ophthalmology.

Mind Control and Meditation

Controlling your mental state is an inexact science, some days it will be easy, other days your attempts will feel useless. Progress in mind control is a slow process, but the rewards are absolutely worth the effort. While, discipline exists without extensive practice in mind-control, you are doing yourself a disservice if you don't do at least some meditative exercises.

Mind-control, as it is defined in this book, is your ability to manage your overall mental state. This means not only knowing how to calm yourself, but also how to go into fight or flight mode when it is appropriate.

When you think of someone who can control their mental state, you might picture a meditation master who has been living in the mountains for decades, but there are many other types of mind-control practices.

A professional strongman needs to put himself into a frenzy in order to deadlift 450 KG, a free diver needs to minimize non-essential physiological functions in order to preserve oxygen, and many great thinkers have unique systems for coming up with their ideas.

Thomas Edison was known to take naps with metal balls in each hand. When he was about to fall asleep, the balls would fall onto metal saucers which had been placed underneath his hands and would cause a loud noise which would wake him up immediately. Edison knew that this state was especially creative. Using his unique method, Edison solved many technical problems and contributed to a number of his inventions.

SELF-DISCIPLINE: THE ART OF BECOMING MORE HUMAN

Meditation is a broad set of systems and techniques with a variety of different goals, including understanding the nature of consciousness, improving awareness, relaxation, emotional control, and achieving enlightenment. There are many different forms of meditation, some examples include Vipassana meditation, Kundalini Yoga, mindfulness meditation, self-hypnosis, and walking meditation. Practicing some form of meditation will substantially enhance your self-discipline and self-knowledge.

You can teach yourself meditation without a guide, or you can employ a specific practice. Since there are so many different schools of meditation, it can be difficult knowing where to start. The following is an excellent meditative technique which will improve your overall mental control in addition to providing other benefits

Every time you meditate, you should practice the following four steps.

1) Sit cross-legged with your back straight, close your eyes, and start taking deep breaths into your lower abdomen. If you are unable to sit cross-legged, sit with your back straight on a flat chair.

2) Observe whatever thoughts appear and then let them go, Observe whatever images appear in your mind's eye, pay attention to the physical sensations in your body (pain in your back, tingling in your fingertips, coldness in your feet) and then let those sensations go.

3) Pay attention to whatever mental states appear; do you experience anger, fear, boredom, anxiety? Let each of these mental states go until you reach a state of empty mind, also known as pure consciousness, no mind, or no thoughts.

4) If you fall out of empty mind and find yourself caught in a stream of images, thoughts, or sensations, let go and go back into empty mind. Note: the challenge is not going back into empty mind, but rather recognizing that you have left the state. What tends to happen is that meditators don't even realize that they have gotten lost in their thoughts.

Don't worry if you can't make it all the way through every step; some people will get stuck at step 1 or step 2 at first. Even if you aren't making it all the way to step 3 and 4 you are still going to experience the mind control benefits of meditation. Just keep practicing, 5 minutes a day is fine, and more than that is great as well.

Experienced meditators will be able to enter pure consciousness much more quickly than beginning meditators. If you are in a hurry or are meditating in a busy public place, you can meditate until you reach pure consciousness and then stay there until you fall out. Once you fall out of pure consciousness, go back to whatever you were doing before meditating. These brief meditation sessions are emotionally and mentally energizing.

"In the province of the mind, what one believes to be true is true or becomes true, within certain limits to be found experientially and experimentally. These limits are further beliefs to be transcended. In the mind, there are no limits."

John Lilly

Mind Control is fundamentally different from discipline. Discipline is more straightforward, you can force yourself to do something, but you can't force yourself into a particular mental state. Developing mind control is much more subtle.

To illustrate this point, try not thinking of a purple hippopotamus.

Most people get a purple hippopotamus stuck in their mind. You can try to get rid of it, but your efforts will backfire making the purple hippopotamus even more persistent. Instead of trying to force it out of your mind, you will need to let it go.

Experienced meditators should be able to do this fairly easily. In fact, experienced meditators should be able to let go of just about any negative thought or image. However, no matter your level of meditation practice, you will likely still encounter the occasional persistent neurotic thought.

The most effective way to overcome a disturbing thought that you can't shake is to remember that it isn't you. Your anxiety isn't you; your anger isn't you, your sadness isn't you. Occasionally, people will say things like "I am angry," but the truth is that this anger is a choice. They are experiencing anger and choosing to identify with it. If you choose not to identify with an unwanted emotion simply accept that it exists, experience it, and recognize that it isn't you, soon the unwanted feeling will disappear.

To be clear, meditation trains general mind control, not specific mind control. If you have some particular mental state, you want to reach or avoid you need specific training.

Want to reduce anxiety? Do things that scare you every day.

Need more energy? Practice high energy activities such as dancing, heavy weight lifting, or stand up comedy.

Another very effective way to develop mind control is through physical exercise. Any kind of exercise will improve your discipline, motivation, energy, and ability to focus, but different kinds of exercise do train mind control in different ways.

Hill sprints, and other forms of high-intensity interval training, develop mind control in an interesting way. When you do hill sprints, you should push very hard on the way up the hill and then usually walk or jog back down depending on your fitness level.

One of the awesome benefits of hill sprints is the way that they train you to quickly return to a relaxed state of mind. By the time you reach the top of the hill, you should be breathing heavy, and your heart should be racing. On the way down, you need to relax and hopefully get back to a reasonable heart rate and breathing pattern by the time you reach the bottom.

If you do 5-10 hill sprints each session, you will get a lot of practice quickly calming yourself from a very intense physiological state. Heavy weight lifting trains your mind in the opposite way; it teaches you how to generate energy and intentionally enter fight or flight.

Any kind of very long endurance activity will train your pain tolerance, but a lot of people don't realize that it also has the potential to improve your ability to remain calm. For example, watch elite distance runners in the first half of the race; they are conserving as much energy as possible while maintaining their speed. In running, or any other endurance sport, a big part of energy conservation is staying relaxed. Many amateur runners will actually burn themselves out psychologically in the first half of the race, not realizing that a big part of endurance is staying as relaxed as possible.

Competitive sports (particularly martial arts) give you more control over your fight or flight state and how to remain rational while your body is producing a lot of adrenaline. In a crisis situation, such as a natural disaster, house fire, or a physical assault, it is very common for people to overreact or even freeze. People who have experience competing in martial arts are much more likely to make the right decision during a dangerous event. That being said, you never know how you will react during a crisis unless you have actually been in a crisis.

EVAN RAYMER

6. Strength Training Principles Applied to Discipline

As mentioned earlier, discipline is like a muscle. So in order to improve your discipline it makes sense to train it like a muscle. Unbeknownst to many people outside of the strength training world, programming for muscular strength is actually a complicated process. This might seem counterintuitive and contrary to your experience; many people believe that if you want to get stronger at some exercise simply perform that exercise frequently.

And this works... until it doesn't. Eventually, trainees will reach a plateau where they can't make progress without more sophisticated planning. Strength athletes are generally categorized into beginner, intermediate, advanced, and elite. Where the more experienced an athlete is, the more complex their programming needs to be.

Different definitions of the term beginner get thrown about. One very common definition is that a beginner is a strength athlete who is able to make progress every session in the gym. Generally speaking, an intermediate is someone who can make progress every week, and an advanced athlete is happy to make progress once a month.

It is important to note that beginner, intermediate, advanced, and elite, don't depend on strength levels, but rather refer to how difficult it is to make progress.

Discipline operates in a similar way. If you are a beginner in your discipline you don't need any special programming at all. Just start doing uncomfortable things, and you will notice rapid gains in your discipline levels. Similarly, intermediates don't necessarily need special programming; however, it can help in certain situations.

A simple strength training program is called linear progression. There are a number of different ways to apply this program; however, we will be using the simplest version to make it easier to apply to self-discipline.

Strength training programs focus on a number of different exercises aimed at developing the entire body, but for the sake of illustrating this point, we will focus on one exercise, the squat. For the following program, the trainee will be doing five sets of five repetitions every session. A repetition means performing the exercise one time, so five repetitions means performing the exercise five times. A set is a series of repetitions with breaks in between, so five sets of five repetitions means doing five squats five times taking breaks in between.

Session 1: 200 lbs

Session 2: 205 lbs

Session 3: 210 lbs

Session 4: 215 lbs

Session 5: 220 lbs

Session 6: 225 lbs

Session 7: 230 lbs

Session 8: 235 lbs

Session 9: 240 lbs

Session 10: 245 lbs

Session 11: 250 lbs

Session 12: 255 lbs

After the end of this series, the trainee could restart the program at 220 lbs and aim to finish their twelve session cycle using 275 lbs. Note: this is just an example and not necessarily recommended in actual practice.

You can apply a very similar type of program to discipline

Let's say you are a salesperson, and you set your own hours. You want to put more time into your work but tend to get exhausted after about eight hours of work in one day. There is always more work to do, such as cold calling people, studying sales tactics, searching for better wholesale prices, etc. You know you need more discipline for work and want to earn more money for yourself or for your family.

You decide that ten hours of work six days per week would be ideal. It would mean enough money, and it would also give you enough free time to do other things. The following cycle will help you progress towards your goal

Since you tend to get exhausted at around eight hours of work per day, we are going to start the Training cycle at 6 hours per day.

Week 1: work 6 hours per day, taking one day off each week.
Week 2: work 6.5 hours per day, taking one day off each week.
Week 3: work 7 hours per day, taking one day off each week.
Week 4: work 7.5 hours per day, taking one day off each week.
Week 5: work 8 hours per day, taking one day off each week.
Week 6: work 8.5 hours per day, taking one day off each week.
Week 7: work 9 hours per day, taking one day off each week.
Week 8: work 9.5 hours per day, taking one day off each week.

After this cycle is completed restart, but this time you can begin with 6.5 or 7 hours per day. Keep repeating the cycle until you successfully finish the 8 week cycle at twelve hours of work per day. Once you have reached this level you should be able to comfortably manage 10 hours per day without a tremendous amount of stress.

Why not just build up to 10 hours per day and maintain there? In strength training programs as well as in discipline, your peak is usually not maintainable. You want to peak well past the level which you plan on maintaining. Want to be able to squat 315 lbs on any given day? You should squat at least 365 lbs at least one time in your life. Want to be able to work for 10 hours every single day? You should be able to maintain 12 hours per day for an entire week at least once.

Strength training coaches discovered that they can push their athletes to new levels by having them follow this kind of ramping up peaking program. Yes, peaking is great for competition, but it also improves overall strength because the athlete is forced to adapt to loads which they normally wouldn't be able to tolerate.

There are plenty of other ways to program for strength training; however it is unclear whether more complexity is necessary when it comes to self-discipline. The following is a twelve-week variation on the above program which might be useful for people with very advanced discipline or who simply prefer a bit of variety.

Week 1: work 6 hours per day, taking one day off each week.

Week 2: work 6.5 hours per day, taking one day off each week.

Week 3: work 7 hours per day, taking one day off each week.

Week 4 (reduce load): work 6.5 hours per day, taking one day off each week.

Week 5: work 7 hours per day, taking one day off each week.

Week 6: work 7.5 hours per day, taking one day off each week.

Week 7: work 8 hours per day, taking one day off each week.

Week 8 (reduce load): work 7.5 hours per day, taking one day off each week.

Week 9: work 8 hours per day, taking one day off each week.

Week 10: work 8.5 hours per day, taking one day off each week.

Week 11: work 9 hours per day, taking one day off each week.

Week 12: work 9.5 hours per day, taking one day off each week.

People with more advanced discipline need more time to make improvements. Notice how in both programs you end up with 9.5 hours per day, but in the second program, it takes twelve weeks instead of eight weeks to reach this level.

At first, you should use the 8-week training program, but if that stops working, you can use the 12-week cycle or even develop your own more advanced cycles.

Another principle in strength training (and sports training in general) is that as an athlete progresses, they need to be more specific in their focus. A beginner strength athlete is able to progress in all of their exercises all at once; on the other hand, a more advanced athlete will need to focus on certain movements while maintaining others.

A similar phenomena exists with discipline. Have you or someone you know rapidly and drastically turned their life around completely after some kind of transformative experience? This is possible because a beginner can improve every aspect of their life all at once, however, as one progresses through their discipline journey, it makes more sense to focus on one or two changes at a time.

If you are advanced in your discipline and trying to improve your performance at work, it might backfire if you try to make too many changes at the same time.

There is one exception to the rule that you shouldn't take on a lot of different changes at once. This is when your life is undergoing a huge transformation. For example, moving to a new city or getting a new job. In this case, you will want to start developing a number of new habits all at once in order to optimize your new routine as quickly as possible.

It is also worth noting that rather than having just a single objective, it is realistic (and arguably a good idea) to have two separate objectives. The reason why is explained in a later section. However, having more than two objectives is likely to cause more harm than good.

Strength training programs inspired much of the Discipline Training Program chapter. In that chapter, you will find a number of different training programs for a whole host of goals.

The Importance of Maintenance

Since the recommended strategy is to focus on one or two aspects of discipline at a time, it is necessarily important to always include a maintenance strategy.

When an advanced strength athlete decides to focus on their overhead pressing ability, they can't afford to lose their deadlift or front squat strength. If they put all their energy into overhead pressing and none of it into anything else they will lose strength in the other movements.

The good news is that it doesn't require much to maintain. The athlete can improve overhead pressing strength while doing just enough repetitions to keep their strength in the rest of their exercises.

The same can be said for discipline. When you are trying to improve your performance at work or in your business, make sure to maintain your fitness, your meditation practice, and your self-education at the same time.

The following is an example of a protocol which could accompany the 8 week work cycle mentioned earlier. Your own maintenance protocol will depend on the habits you have already developed.

1) Meditate for 5 minutes upon waking every single morning. You don't need to meditate for long periods of time to reap tremendous rewards. It's fine to make the goal 10 or 15 minutes instead of 5, but the main priority of this maintenance program is to be very manageable and robust.

2) Exercise for 45 minutes three times per week. The type of exercise will depend on what you have been doing in the past. Do the same kind of movements that you are used to doing, don't do something brand new. If you prefer to work out more often that is fine as well.

3) If you have some kind of self-education plan, maintain that. Spending a few minutes every day learning something new will be enough to keep self-education at the same level for most people.

Two Goals are Sometimes Better than One

While having a singular focus works for many people, some of us are actually better off having two separate goals. If you put all of your mental energy and identity into one thing, and it doesn't go according to plan, this could cause major disruptions in your identity and potentially result in depressive symptoms.

For people who are susceptible to depression or are generally emotionally unstable, it is preferable to have two simultaneous goals at any given time. If someone puts all of their energy into a business which eventually fails, this might set them back for a while psychologically. But, if they were also training for a marathon at the same time at least, they would have some kind of backup plan for their identity.

This doesn't mean that you can't focus more energy into one of your two goals, nor does it mean that both goals have to be equally important. In fact, it probably makes sense to see one of your two goals as an extra, somewhere to go if the main goal doesn't go well.

If you focus all of your energy onto one primary goal you may end up feeling drained. As a result, when you've completed everything you need to do, there is a good chance that instead of doing something interesting or productive, you default to wasting your time on youtube, social media, or watching television.

This is another reason to include a secondary goal. It gives you an additional purpose when you are tired of pursuing your main goal. Instead of wasting your extra time when you are done pursuing your main goal for the day, you can use that extra time in a more valuable and interesting way.

EVAN RAYMER

7. DISCIPLINE AND TIME SCALES

A physical muscle can be trained for short term power, a middle-distance pace, or longer endurance. When performing a weight lifting exercise, there is an inverse relationship between the weight on the bar and the number of reps performed. For example, let's say someone can bench press 80 kilos for a maximum of 10 reps, this same person will likely be able to bench press 100 kilos for only 1 or 2 reps, but might be able to bench press 30 kilos for 100 reps.

There is a similar relationship between force of discipline and the amount of time discipline can be sustained. I.e. the more effort needed to sustain a certain amount of discipline the less time that effort can be maintained.

Imagine an activity which requires an intense degree of focus, for example, learning advanced math or playing blindfold chess. Most people will struggle to maintain this level of focus for more than a couple of hours, in fact, many people can't hold this level of focus for more than a couple of minutes. Even if a well-practiced expert is able to maintain the necessary level of focus for more than a few hours they are likely to be drained afterwards. This form of discipline is called short-term discipline. Short-term discipline lasts anywhere from a few seconds to a couple of weeks.

The next discipline time frame exists in between short-term discipline and long-term discipline, it is called middle-distance discipline. This form of discipline involves following a medium-term plan, the execution of which lasts anywhere from a couple of weeks to a few months. An example of middle-distance discipline would be an already fit person training for a half marathon. This requires creating a training plan and sticking to it over the course of a couple of months, depending on the person's previous experience running. It's easier to stick with a difficult running program over the course of two months than it is to stick to the same program over the course of two years. While following a plan is an important part of discipline, it's not necessary that you create the plan yourself. Sometimes it will make more sense for you to design the plan, and in other situations, it will make more sense to get assistance from someone with more expertise. What's important with respect to discipline is that you carry out the plan as intended.

Long-term discipline involves executing any plan which lasts longer than a couple of months. A perfect example of long-term discipline is saving money for retirement. It's very easy to live on a budget for one day, but few people can maintain their budget or saving goals for 20 years.

It's certainly possible to have discipline at all three-time scales; in fact, that is the ideal. Like a resilient athlete, you want to have both strength and endurance. However, most readers will find that at least one of these three-time scales of discipline comes naturally to them, and at least one of these three-time scales of discipline is more difficult.

Short-term Discipline

Reaching peak levels of short-term discipline usually requires motivation or a substantial degree of mind control. People who have a high degree of short-term discipline are sometimes very emotional. Over the course of their lives, they have learned how to channel their emotions into unbelievable performances.

People who struggle with short-term discipline are usually more mild-mannered and stable. They might have excellent long-term discipline, but are unable to draw up the intensity for a short sprint. The way to improve short-term discipline is through mind-control exercises. Find certain cues which trigger emotional intensity. For example, some people find that thinking about their mortality can produce a strong emotional reaction which puts them into performance mode.

It is possible that you struggle with short-term discipline for the opposite reason. Not because you are unemotional and cold, but rather because you are overly emotional and unable to concentrate due to being overwhelmed. If this is the case, the best antidote is to meditate daily. Another thing to do is to inoculate yourself to stressful situations. Find experiences, actions, or situations which scare you and pursue them head-on. A weakness in short-term discipline may be a result of a shortcoming in pain tolerance, focus, and/or courage/vulnerability. Sometimes sprint-discipline relies on a substantial amount of pain tolerance; this is particularly important in physical competition or performance.

An inability to focus is usually the reason why someone lacks in sprint discipline. If you need to perform well on a standardized test or to quickly finish a project at work, you will need to muster up a high intensity of focus. Even in physical competition focus is extremely important.

A lack of courage/vulnerability can occasionally be the source of a weakness in sprint discipline. The soldier who risks his own life to save his teammate displays a tremendous degree of courage/vulnerability. The soldier who abandons his teammates in favor of self-preservation displays the opposite.

If you lack in short-term discipline, look for the source of this weakness. There is more information on how to improve each kind of discipline in the respective sections.

MIDDLE-DISTANCE DISCIPLINE

This discipline time-frame involves following medium-term plans, generally between a few weeks to a few months. In order to accomplish most goals it is necessary to chunk effort into blocks.

If you are training to run a marathon in six months, it will make sense to break up your training plan into a series of cycles instead of planning it all at once. It's hard to know how quickly you will progress, especially if you are a beginner runner, so it doesn't make sense to plan out how many kilometers you will be running on day 147. Instead, create a plan for the first three weeks, and then after observing the results, you can reevaluate and develop a strategy for a new training block.

If you are writing a book, it is best to break it up into blocks as well. For example: first, create a research and planning block where you develop ideas and design a structure for your book. The amount of time required for this block will depend on your research requirements. Let's say you give yourself a month for research and planning. In this block, you are required to read for 3 hours a day and plan for an hour a day.

Next, you could plan one or multiple writing blocks where you create your first draft. Many writers find that 1000 words per day is a good goal. Some writers find that they can do a lot more than 1000 words, and others prefer to aim for 500 words per day. If you write at least 1000 words each day, you will have a 60 000 word first draft in less than 2 months.

Finally, plan out an editing block. Let's say you give yourself a month to edit and work for a minimum of 4 hours per day editing. In this particular example, you will have written a well researched, well-written, well-edited book in only 4 months.

If you or someone else are able to break up a project into blocks and you have sufficient middle-distance discipline to implement the plan, you will be able to efficiently and effectively execute on a number of different projects.

There are many ways to improve your middle-distance discipline. The first is very easy, it is a simple cognitive switch. Instead of focusing on large projects which will take more than a few months, break the project into parts and focus on each part one at a time. If you don't feel competent breaking your project into parts, find someone who can.

Another way to improve your middle-distance discipline is to practice following through with your blocks. This may be difficult at first, but over time, you will improve substantially. It is easier to improve your middle-distance discipline than it is to improve your short-term discipline or your long-term discipline.

The training programs described later on in this book require middle-distance discipline to implement. By design, they are mostly eight weeks long. Eight weeks is an excellent standard option for a training block. It's long enough to make some serious progress, but also short enough for your life to be predictable.

In addition to being perfect for training for competition and working on projects like writing a book, middle-distance discipline is what you need to develop new habits. If you want to start meditating, hitting the gym, or eating healthier food, use a middle-distance plan to create the habit and then use long-distance discipline to maintain the habit.

A weakness in middle-distance discipline could be the result of a problem in resistance to temptation, courage/vulnerability, or initiation.

Resistance to temptation is occasionally the source of a problem with middle-distance discipline. This is particularly common when someone is trying to improve their eating habits.

Most of the time middle-distance discipline is necessary for trying something new. If you are entering into a new environment, learning a new skill, and/or interacting with a new group of people, some amount of courage/vulnerability is necessary.

Initiation is often the reason why you might struggle with middle-distance discipline. Many of the plans involved in middle-distance discipline require getting to work on some kind of activity. A weakness in initiation means that getting to work is more difficult.

For more information on improving these different forms of discipline, check the respective sections.

LONG-DISTANCE DISCIPLINE

Lasting anywhere from a couple of months to years and even decades, long-distance discipline is the most challenging form of discipline for a lot of people. The more time that passes, the more likely you are to have a very low motivation day which somehow sabotages your goals. This is why long-term goals need to be more modest and more robust.

A classic example of a challenging long-term goal is staying healthy. Many people can follow a diet for a few months, but staying healthy for the rest of your life is much more tricky. Trying to eat exclusively healthy foods for the rest of your life is not a robust goal for most people. At some point, they are likely to break the commitment. On the other hand, eating healthy 90 percent of the time is something most people are capable of doing. You might wonder why not try to eat as healthy as possible all the time. Actually this is a smart thing to do, you should try to eat as healthy as you can. Just don't make it a definite-goal to eat healthy all the time. Most people will eventually slip up and as mentioned earlier you don't ever want to commit to a goal and not complete it.

Sticking to a very intense exercise regimen for the rest of your life may not be a realistic goal. However, for most people, it is realistic to say "I will exercise six days a week for the rest of my life, even if I feel bad or if I am sick I will at least go for a walk or do something small." It's not hard to exercise every single day no matter how bad you feel, but if your goal is to run a half-marathon every day, chances are you will eventually give in and break your self-commitment.

Make your health goals robust by leaving some room for flexibility. In the short-term and middle-distance discipline range you can create more strict and more ambitious goals, but for the very long-run it's best to give yourself some room to maneuver.

Saving money over the long-term is a tricky goal because a single bad decision can set you back a long-way. Trying to save half your pay cheque over the long-run probably isn't realistic, but a lot of people are able to save 10 percent of what they earn. Sure, plenty of people are able to save half their paycheque or even 90 percent of their paycheque over the course of a couple of months, but this isn't a good idea as a long-term goal. Chances are at some point you won't reach your savings goal. It's much better to set a more modest objective

Improving long-distance discipline involves setting robust and realistic goals which can be maintained over the long-term. Since these goals are reasonable and robust enough to be maintained you need to develop a habit of sticking to them no matter how unmotivated you feel.

If you struggle with long-term discipline, you likely need to improve your patience, your tolerance for boredom, and possibly your resistance to temptation as well.

All long-term goals require patience. The natural tendency is to give up and refocus your efforts onto something with more immediate rewards. Patience gives you the ability to withstand this impulse and stay on the right path.

Certain long-term goals, particularly skill development, rely on tolerance for boredom. Learning a skill can be fun and engaging, but just as often it is dull and uninteresting. If you lack in long-term discipline, consider that your weakness might be stemming from your inability to tolerate boredom.

Occasionally, a weakness in resistance to temptation is the reason why someone lacks in long-term discipline. For many long-term goals, there are certain temptations which interfere with successfully achieving the objective. For example, temptations to spend money could interfere with your ability to save for retirement.

If you have a problem with long-term discipline, you will never achieve your true potential. Diagnose the type of discipline or disciplines which are the source of your problem, read that section, and then apply the recommended techniques to improve yourself.

EVAN RAYMER

8. Discipline Training Programs

While some people will find the information in the previous chapters sufficient to create their own training programs, other people will prefer to have some clear instructions in terms of how they can improve their discipline. This section includes a number of different training protocols for improving discipline in different ways.

Each of the protocols is designed for either beginner, intermediate, advanced, or for all levels.

A beginner is someone who doesn't have a meditation practice, doesn't exercise consistently, is unemployed or struggles to meet the work demands of their job or business, rarely educates themselves, and gives into temptation regularly.

An intermediate has some kind of consistent meditation practice, a consistent exercise routine regularly educates themselves by reading or through another method, maintains their job or business comfortably, and only occasionally gives into temptation.

Someone with advanced discipline has a well developed meditation practice which they never skip, has a very consistent intensive exercise routine, educates themselves daily, surpasses expectations at their job or in their business, almost never gives into temptation and if they do it is in moderation.

Note: it is certainly possible to be a beginner in one part of life and to be advanced in another. For example, someone could have a very consistent meditation practice and maintain their fitness, but at the same time, they might be underperforming at their job. The good news is that they don't have far to go. If they implement a couple of training programs related to work they will be performing beyond their expectations.

In all of the following programs, you are meant to maintain the habits you develop during the program throughout the entire course of the program. So if it says to do something in weeks 1 and 2, that doesn't mean you get to stop doing it in weeks 3 and 4, you are supposed to keep doing it all the way until the final week.

After the program is over, unless otherwise specified, it is a good idea to maintain whatever habits you acquired throughout the course of the program. These habits should be fairly well established after 8 weeks of intense focus. You can now take a few weeks to deload or go straight into another 8 week program.

Any time you use some measurement as a yardstick for success, you will start experiencing problems. If your goal in the gym is to lift heavier weights, there will be a tendency to sacrifice technique in order to move heavier weights. If you make your goal earning more money, you will be inclined to forego other goals in favor of the bottom line. In these programs, the goals are related to time spent doing the activity. This is likely the least problematic measurement for progress. That being said, measuring the time spent doing the activity fails to consider how the actual activity is performed. With that in mind, try your best to work within the spirit of the programs. Most of the programs aren't particularly demanding, you should be able to maintain technique, awareness, and intensity of focus throughout.

Because readers come from all different walks of life, the majority of the following programs are designed for people who have other commitments. If you are unemployed, work part-time, or even work full-time without a lot of activities outside of work, feel free to increase the workload on any of these programs (except the fitness program).

However, if you are fairly inexperienced when it comes to improving your discipline, it is recommended to follow at least one 8 week program word for word. This way, you can get a better sense of what you are capable of. You might find the program more difficult than you expected. If you were able to make it to the end of the program without missing a single day, feel free to make your next program more intense.

Mind Control Program for Beginners

As mentioned in a previous chapter, mind control is a very useful pursuit to train alongside discipline. It is the ability to consciously change or control your mental state. People have been using a number of different mind control techniques for millennia. Currently, we are blessed with the knowledge gained through thousands of years of trial and error. The following program is ideal for someone who is new to meditation and other forms of mind control. It won't turn you into a master meditator in only 8 weeks, but it will give you strong habits which you will be able to maintain for a long time.

Weeks 1 and 2:

15 minutes of meditation first thing every morning. For more information on how to meditate see the chapter on meditation and mind control.

Weeks 3 and 4:

30 minutes of hill runs 3 times per week. Run up the hill and walk or run slowly on the way down. It doesn't matter how big or how steep the hill is, you can run up small hills faster and bigger hills more slowly. Aim to stay relaxed on the way up and calm yourself on the way down. This exercise will teach you to control your emotions during a physiologically aroused state.

You should feel refreshed by the time you reach the bottom of the hill. If you are still huffing and puffing at the bottom, you should find a way to reduce the intensity. You can do this by moving more slowly on the way down, running more slowly on the way up, or even walking up part of the way.

If there are no hills near you or you are physically incapable of running up hills then you can try another form of high-intensity interval training. Good options include kettlebells, swimming, cycling, running stairs, or high-intensity sports.

Remember, the point of this exercise is to develop mind control and not to improve your fitness. Your fitness will likely improve in the process, but this is a positive side effect and not the main point.

Note: hill running and other forms of high-intensity interval training are physiologically demanding, and you should consult a medical professional before attempting this training program.

Weeks 5 and 6:

Add an additional 15 minute meditation session at some point during the day every single day. This can be right before bed, in the afternoon, or whenever is convenient for you.

Weeks 7 and 8:

Increase to five 30-minute hill running sessions per week. Feel free to substitute these sessions with something else if necessary.

Post:

After this 8 week program, beginners should have experienced substantial improvements in their mind-control. In addition to other benefits, you will be able to focus more effectively, relax more easily in a stressful situation, and learn to detach more effectively from your thoughts and emotions. However, the true program benefits won't emerge until you have maintained the habits for years. If you can maintain these meditation habits for a long time, you will transform the way your mind works.

Fitness Training Program for Beginners

Having a basic fitness regimen is important for anyone who is on a quest to become more disciplined. It teaches pain tolerance, tolerance for boredom, and it improves mind-control.

The following training program is designed for people who currently don't have any kind of fitness program. By sticking to this program, you will not only experience benefits in your physical fitness, but you will also experience improvements in your motivation, focus, and general energy.

Note: There are potential safety risks in any kind of physical training routine. Consult a medical professional before attempting this program.

Weeks 1-4:

3 days a week of full-body Strength Training. Perform a lower body strength movement, a pressing strength movement, and a pulling strength movement every single session. These strength movements should be compound exercises, which means that they involve lots of different muscle groups.

Examples of lower body strength movements: back squat, front squat, lunge, sumo deadlift, split squat, and reverse lunge.

Examples of pressing strength movements: bench press, incline bench press, overhead press, pushups, dips, and various dumbbell presses.

Examples of pulling strength movements: pull up, chin up, neutral grip pull up, bent over row, dumbbell row, assisted pull up, and the lat pull down machine.

There are lots of great strength training programs for beginners. Stronglifts 5x5 is an excellent option. All the information you need can be found here https://stronglifts.com/5x5/

Weeks 5-8:

Do some quick active mobility before each Strength Training session. Ideally, you should move all of your joints through their full range of motion. There are lots of reasonable warm-up routines, a great option is Pavel Tsatsouline's *Super Joints*. Your active stretching routine doesn't need to last longer than 10 minutes.

Add 30 minutes of cardio three times per week after your Strength Training sessions. Running, cycling, speed walking, swimming, or rowing are all acceptable options. Don't try to destroy your body. Instead, the idea is to simply stimulate your physiology and burn calories.

Post:

This routine will get you into reasonable shape. If you continue to follow the routine after the 8 weeks are over, you should be strong, flexible, and fit enough to feel comfortable using your body in a variety of different sports and activities. However, if you have any specific goals, such as running a marathon, getting as strong as possible, or competing in a sport, it would make more sense to follow a specific training program and if possible to consult an expert.

Beginner Self-Education Program

Most people understand the value of learning, this can include formal or non-formal education. As technology is progressing, information is becoming increasingly accessible to more and more people and in new innovative ways.

Where in the past information was primarily dispersed through physical books, university lectures, or in face-to-face conversation? We can now watch university lectures online, read ebooks, order physical books straight to our doorstep in a few days, listen to books in audio format, visit informational websites, listen to podcasts, or access the seemingly endless amount of free informational content available on video sharing platforms like YouTube.

Physical books have become a status symbol due to their long history as our main medium of knowledge. However, there is no reason to limit yourself to certain kinds of information sources.

Despite being blessed with this enormous range and quantity of information we are cursed more than ever by distractions. While learning has always required discipline, it requires more discipline now than it ever did before.

If you want to learn in the most efficient way possible, it is important to include two main sources of education into your daily routine. You ought to include some kind of passive learning into your schedule. This means learning while you are doing something else. A straightforward example would be listening to audiobooks or informational podcasts while you are doing chores, driving or running errands. Passive learning is valuable because it allows you to take advantage of mental space, which might not be used otherwise. While an extensive active learning program would be very useful in terms of education, it would also take up a lot of time for people who have other commitments. The main downside of passive learning is that it is difficult to study more difficult topics. Anyone who listens to audiobooks regularly has had the experience of being interrupted at a key moment, or during a difficult concept, of course, the interrupter normally didn't mean to be rude and has no idea how deeply engrossed you were in the book.

Histories, biographies, new languages, popular science, and basic psychology are all great options for passive learning. The best type of passive learning involves concepts which can be understood on their own, i.e., concepts which don't rely on understanding a previous concept. If you are driving and get distracted from your audiobook for 5 minutes, it might be unsafe or impractical to rewind back to the point where you lost track. Every section in the audiobook should make sense on its own.

Active learning is usually more important than passive learning. This is because it allows you to investigate a subject more deeply and understand concepts which build on each other. You can't understand algebra without an excellent understanding of multiplication, division, addition, and subtraction. Additionally, you need a strong command of trigonometry and algebra to understand calculus. Some of the most important knowledge can only be acquired through active learning. You will never learn computer programming while washing the dishes at the same time. In fact, most employable skills can only be acquired through active learning.

The following discipline training program will help you develop daily active and passive learning habits. In this program, you get to choose what you study and what source materials you use. If you are looking to develop an employable skill, study that skill during your active learning sessions. If you don't have a specific employable skill you want to learn, feel free to study and learn whatever excites you intellectually. While it is possible to learn a subject that bores you, the best way to understand something at a deep level is by being intrinsically interested in the topic.

Weeks 1-2:

20 minutes of active learning daily.

Weeks 3-4:

30 minutes of passive learning daily.

Weeks 5-6:

An additional 20 minutes of active learning daily reaching a total of 40 minutes of active learning daily.

Weeks 7-8:

An additional 30 minutes of passive learning daily. Added together this might seem like a lot of time for a beginner program. However, most people have more than an hour of free time most days when they are doing chores, going to the gym, or running errands and could be listening to an audiobook or a podcast at the same time.

Post:

The benefits of learning add up over the course of years. 8 weeks following this program won't give you a deep or broad understanding of much of anything. However, it will give you the habits and discipline necessary to become a lifelong learner. Continue to follow this program or something similar for a couple of years, and you will dramatically improve your education level.

Resistance to Temptation Program - All Levels

Most people have a number of different temptations which do them in on a regular basis. In this program, you are meant to focus on one big temptation throughout the course of the entire program rather than try to eliminate all of your temptations all at once.

After you have eliminated your most pressing and seemingly unbeatable temptation, you can move on to the less sinister temptations and possibly even overcome them in less than 8 weeks. However, for the first resistance to temptation program, you should commit to the total time frame.

There is more specific advice on how to resist temptation in the chapter on the Different Types of Discipline.

First:

Identify the temptation you want to overcome and decide whether it is best to completely eliminate it or to reach a moderate level of consumption. Many alcoholics find that they are better off completely abstaining from alcohol. However, if you have a bad habit of eating too much dessert it might be a bit extreme to completely eliminate cakes from your diet.

Write down your goal, and if at any point during the 8 weeks you give in to your temptation, you must write down an admission of guilt. If you feel up for it you can also force yourself to admit your failure by contacting a friend and letting them know what happened.

Weeks 1-2:

These will be the easiest weeks to avoid temptation. You should feel excited and confident about your goal.

Weeks 3-6:

This is where you are most likely to give in. The initial enthusiasm has been lost, and it feels like you are far away from your objective. This is the point where the subsystems working to sabotage your success become more active, understand that the words in your mind encouraging you to give in are just a trick, do not allow your more sinister subsystems to fool you.

Weeks 7-8:

You made it this far so you might as well go all the way to the end. Your negative behaviour patterns may have given up at this point, recognizing the power of your resolve; on the other hand, they might go on an all-out offensive during the last two weeks. This will depend on how you have acted in the past.

If you have successfully followed through with your self-commitments in the past your negative subsystems will know that any efforts to make you give up at this point are simply a waste of energy. But, if you have given up in the past, these malicious subsystems are more likely to try to take you out right at the end. This is part of the reason why it is so important to follow through with your self-commitments; it shows your negative subsystems that you aren't worth messing with.

Post:

Once you have resisted temptation for 8 weeks, it will be much easier to resist in the future. However, even if it feels like the temptation has been completely beaten back, sometimes it still festers and bides its time in the darkest recesses of your mind. Never underestimate the ability of any temptation to regroup and take you down when you are feeling weak.

IMPROVING A SPECIFIC SKILL

Achieving mastery in any skill may require pain tolerance, courage/vulnerability, resistance to temptation, focus, or initiation depending on the specific skill. However, certainly it requires tolerance for boredom more than anything else. In pursuing any skill some days will be more enjoyable than others. When you are feeling interested and engaged learning the skill won't require much discipline at all, but on those days when you don't feel like putting in the work, that is when tolerance for boredom comes into play. For more information on tolerance for boredom and the flow state, see Chapter 2 on the different types of discipline.

It seems that learning the fundamentals is very important for nearly every kind of skill including martial arts, chess, math, science, music, dance, and writing. Despite this, it is a common mistake to ignore the fundamentals and go straight to the more advanced concepts and techniques.

Beginners should certainly focus on developing the fundamental skills more than anything else, but even if you see yourself as an intermediate or an advanced practitioner, there is a good chance that you could benefit from some additional practice in the most basic aspects of your skill.

The programming in this section includes a substantial amount of fundamentals practice. If you are sure that you are an expert and don't need to work on your fundamentals, feel free to substitute that fundamentals practice for another useful technique or concept.

In addition to practicing the fundamentals, this program also includes a lot of free form practice or playing. Simply follow your whims, your intuitions, and experiment. In the beginning, you are likely to try all kinds of strange, unorthodox things, but after years of free form practice something interesting happens, your free form practice is likely to gradually transform into more orthodox traditional practice. You will, over time and through experience, understand why the traditions of your art exist. These orthodoxies also developed through years of free form practice.

If you are able to come to these traditional conclusions and practices on your own, your understanding of your art will be much deeper. Also, since you have a better understanding of the origin of these practices you will be able to assess which conventions have practical value and which conventions are simply dogmatic.

In every skill or art, intermediate and advanced practitioners tend to reach plateaus, this can be very frustrating because no matter how hard they practice, they can't improve their abilities. One reason why people reach plateaus is that they have lost their Beginner's Mind. Beginner's Mind, known as Shoshin in Zen Buddhism, is a state of mind characterized by enthusiasm, receptivity, modesty, and a lack of preconceptions no matter how much expertise you have already developed. Returning to Beginner's Mind is the most reliable way to break through a plateau in any skill. Part of the reason why you engage in free-form practice and study the fundamentals is to cultivate a state of Beginner's Mind. This will help you progress more efficiently and develop a deeper understanding of whatever skill you are practicing.

The following is a basic framework for improving your abilities in any skill. The time suggestions assume that you have a full-time job and some other commitments so they are not overwhelming. However, if you want to dedicate more time to developing your skill feel free to modify the program to meet your needs.

Weeks 1-2:

Practice the fundamentals of your skill for at least 15 minutes every single day.

Weeks 3-4:

Engage in playful free form practice for at least 20 minutes every single day.

Weeks 5-6:

Practice the fundamentals of your skill for an additional 15 minutes every single day.

Weeks 7-8:

Do free form practice for an additional 20 minutes every single day.

Post:

The more practice you do, the better. In this program, by the time you are in weeks 7-8, you will be engaging in 40 minutes of free form practice and 30 minutes of fundamentals practice every single day. This means an hour and 10 minutes of total practice per day and 8 hours and 10 minutes of practice in total for the entire week. You can certainly do more than this if you have the desire and free time. That being said, this program isn't simply designed to make you an expert in 8 weeks; instead it is meant to help you develop the habits necessary to become an expert over the course of years. Bear in mind that if you set a more ambitious goal, it may be difficult to maintain your habits after the program is over.

Generally speaking, you can't make massive progress in a skill over the course of only eight weeks unless you are a beginner or you spend an inordinate amount of time practicing. For example, if you were to train for 12 hours a day every single day for the entire 8 weeks this would be equivalent to 96 hours per week or 768 total hours practicing. Which would certainly be enough practice to make substantial progress. But, most people simply don't have 12 hours per day to dedicate themselves to practicing a particular skill. This is why, if you want to reach expert level in nearly anything, you must plan on reaching that level over the course of years and not over the course of weeks. Consistent, intentional daily practice over the long-term will turn you into an extremely skilled practitioner. This is why strong habits are more important than 8 weeks of intense focus.

Focus Training Program

For many people focus will be the most important aspect of discipline to develop for their career success. This is particularly true for people working in cognitively demanding industries such as academia, science, writing, law, technology, and engineering.

With social media, email, and on-demand entertainment, focus may be more difficult now than it ever was in human history. However, difficult doesn't mean impossible, and many people are learning to overcome these distractions reaching new impressive heights in their ability to maintain attention. The smartphone may very well be the greatest challenge in your journey to improve focus. After all, some of the greatest minds in the world are working full-time trying to keep you addicted to various different notifications. Before moving on to the training program, here are some things you may want to do if your smartphone is currently interfering with your ability to focus.

1) Turn off all notifications. This doesn't work every time, for some reason with certain apps and certain phones, you can't seem to completely turn off the notifications. If this is the case for you just put your phone on airplane mode.

2) Make your phone difficult to access. While you are working, keep it in a different room inside of a drawer, under a book, and inside of a bag. Temptation is odd in that you are much less likely to give in if giving in requires effort, the more difficult it is for you to access your phone the safer your focus will be.

3) Delete all of your social media applications. You don't have to delete your account (although that is a reasonable option as well). Instead, any time you want to log in simply download the app. When you are done delete the app again. If you have to download the app every time you want to use it you will be much less likely to be tempted to check your notifications when you shouldn't be checking them.

Some purists might criticize these recommendations and argue that your inability to resist the temptation is a failure of discipline rather than a problem with the phone itself. In a literal sense, this criticism is correct, if you had infinite discipline you would be able to resist the urge to check notifications. However, this is a situation where the muscle metaphor applies better than the momentum metaphor. Having to resist the urge to use your phone drains your willpower and the more you can do to reduce this urge, the more discipline you will have for other things. Not to mention the fact that smartphone applications and social media, in particular, are getting more addictive and more effective at controlling your behaviour over time. Yes, if you follow the techniques in this book your discipline will improve. But can your discipline improve as fast as the social media tech giants improve their ability to control your attention?

For the following program, you ought to choose a mentally challenging goal which requires a lot of focus. You can pick something pragmatic involving your work, something creative such as producing a musical album, or something which interests you purely for its own sake, e.g. chess. This program will not only mean immediate progress in your goal, but it will also help you develop the habits necessary to improve your more general focus over the long-term. This program is designed for someone who has a full-time job and other responsibilities. If you have more free time or are able to do this program during your working hours, feel free to do substantially more than the program suggests.

Weeks 1-2:

Spend 30 unbroken minutes every day working on your project. If during this time you get distracted and do something else, write down the date and what distracted you. You can use a code to speed up the process if you want. For example, March 13 YT*1 (March 13th was distracted by Youtube 1 time). The embarrassment of having to write down every failure to maintain focus should be enough to keep you on task nearly every time. If it isn't enough, commit to showing your results to a friend.

Weeks 3-4:

One 20 minute session of productive meditation session every single day. Each time choose something which contributes to the overall goal you chose for this program. For more instructions on Cal Newport's productive meditation, see the section on focus in Chapter 2.

Weeks 5-6:

Increase to a full hour of unbroken time working on your project every day. Continue to record any time you get distracted.

Weeks 7-8:

Add an additional 20 minutes of productive meditation every single day. This could be a second 20-minute session, or you can do it all in one 40 minute chunk.

Post:

While some people will notice massive improvements during the 8 week program, this alone may not be enough to substantially increase your focus over the long-term. Improvements in focus sometimes take a very long time. That being said, this program will give you a set of habits, which if maintained, will improve your focus substantially over the course of a year.

SAMPLE COURAGE/VULNERABILITY PROGRAM

As mentioned in a previous chapter courage and vulnerability were originally meant to be seperate sections. However, further inspection revealed that they are actually the same thing.

There are a number of situations which can induce a state of fear, anxiety, or insecurity. Some of these situations are likely to apply to you, and others won't. Since everyone has different triggers for fear, anxiety, and insecurity you will need a specific protocol to get over your own. This section features an example you can use to model your own program.

For your own Courage/Vulnerability program, you ought to choose the activity which causes you the most discomfort, tests your courage, and your ability to handle vulnerability. This could include various kinds of social situations, dating, public speaking, heights, or other phobias. For other activities which cause less discomfort, feel free to dedicate less than 8 weeks, but for the first time, it is best to do a full 8 week program. After observing the results, you will have a better sense of how to plan your next program and how long you actually need.

For the sample program, we will be working on social anxiety. Most people experience social anxiety to at least some extent, so it is an insecurity which many people can at least partially relate to. It is important to note that some people actually have an extreme paralyzing level of social anxiety, which would be better served by a professional. The following program is certainly not meant to be a substitute for professional attention.

Weeks 1-2:

Engage in at least one interaction with someone you don't know every single day. This could include talking to a stranger in the elevator, starting a conversation on the bus, or going to a party with people you don't know.

Weeks 3-4:

Each week have at least one twenty-minute long (or longer) conversation with a stranger or someone whom you wouldn't have spent much time with before. If this seems difficult to arrange remember that you are starting conversations with strangers every single day, chances are that you will get along with at least some of these people. If none of the conversations with strangers pan out consider contacting an old school acquaintance or a former work colleague.

During your twenty-minute long conversation, try to talk about something unique or personal. Avoid bland or impersonal topics like the weather, news, or politics. Good conversation topics include philosophy, spirituality, and personal dreams/goals. Sticking to bland conversations or socially accepted opinions will preserve and enable social anxiety. Also, absolutely do not pre-plan the things that you are going to say, this is a defense mechanism which prevents you from addressing social anxiety directly.

Weeks 5-6

Increase to a total of twelve conversations with strangers each week. It doesn't matter how long these conversations last.

Weeks 7-8

Have at least 2 twenty-minute long (or longer) conversations with strangers or people whom you don't know well.

Post:

This program should transform your sense of social anxiety and permanently change the way you interact with other people. Unlike some of the other programs, you don't need to maintain your habits after this program is over. But, it would be a good idea to regularly associate with strangers or with people who you don't know well. If social anxiety isn't a major problem for you, you can still use the previous outline to create your own program for your own insecurities. Unlike other forms of discipline which require consistent long-term work, insecurities and fears should be attacked in an intense, focused, short-term approach. After your courage/vulnerability program is over, you don't need to maintain the habits to sustain the benefits.

Perform Better at Work

Many people have misgivings about the idea of putting extra effort into performing better at their jobs. Perhaps they feel a certain degree of bitterness for the fact that they have to show up and do things they don't feel like doing every single day.

What these people forget is that even if they don't enjoy their work, they did accept this job because of the security it provides. While working for yourself is rewarding, liberating, and potentially more profitable, it can also be risky and stressful.

If you work for yourself you can modify this program or you can look at the brief outline in the section on strength training and discipline. Business owners and independent contractors all have many things that they can do to improve their performance.

However, no matter how much work you do, no matter how much you educate yourself in your free time, and no matter who you befriend at the workplace there is no way to guarantee a promotion.

There are a number of different factors out of your control which impact who gets promoted or if anyone gets promoted at all. That being said, the best way to put yourself in a position for a promotion is by performing your job to the best of your ability. No matter who likes or dislikes you, strong performance can't be denied. The following program won't guarantee any particular position in your company. But, it will maximize your chances of being considered for a higher responsibility role if that is something you are looking for. Even if you aren't looking for a promotion putting in your absolute best effort is still recommended. It increases your job security and it is good for the company as well.

Note: This program suggests showing up early for work and staying late every single day. You should be spending this time getting work done. Since you are less likely to be distracted during this time, you may be able to concentrate on important tasks which you normally wouldn't be able to focus on.

Weeks 1-3:

Show up for work 15 minutes early and stay 15 minutes late every single day. If you aren't allowed in the building early spend 30 minutes each working day studying something which will make you better at your job.

Weeks 4-6:

Spend 30 minutes every working day studying something which will make you better at your job in your own free time. Alternatively, spend 30 minutes every workday engaged on a project relevant to your job.

Weeks 7-8:

Arrive at work an additional 15 minutes earlier and stay an additional 15 minutes later. If you aren't allowed in the building during these times, spend 30 minutes every working day studying something relevant to your job.

Post:

By the end of this program, you will be arriving at work 30 minutes earlier, staying 30 minutes later, and spending an additional

30 minutes every working day studying or working on a project relevant to your job.

Following this program alone won't substantially improve your performance at work, but it will give you the habits you need to become an excellent employee. Don't follow the program for 8 weeks and then give up; this will look odd to your coworkers. Instead, look to maintain the routine or something similar to it for years.

Writing Training Program

When some people think of writing and other creative pursuits, they imagine that it requires more inspiration than discipline. This is incorrect. The need for inspiration is an excuse to avoid putting in the necessary work. If you sit down and start writing without distractions, inspiration will come to you eventually. This program specifically focuses on writing; however, it applies to many other creative pursuits. For painting, music, film, etc. use the program outline and modify it to fit the specific requirements of your craft.

In terms of writing three forms of discipline are critical.

The first is initiation. Writers and creative types, in general, understand that getting started is often the most difficult part of a creative project. Some writers even go as far as to say that getting started is the only challenging aspect of writing. The best way to overcome the initiation hurdle is by having a routine. Write in a specific place and at a specific time. If possible write when everyone else is asleep. Many prolific writers get up very early or stay up very late.

One reason why people struggle getting started is that the whole project seems overwhelming. They can't imagine actually writing an entire book or even an entire article. If this is your problem set an easy daily goal for yourself. Some writers will aim for a minimum of 500 words per day, others prefer 1000 per day. Choose a modest goal you know that you can meet no matter how tired or uninspired you feel. Let's say you choose to write a minimum of 500 words per day. On a bad day, you just barely make your goal. But, on a good day, when you are feeling motivated and inspired, you write for four hours straight and actually manage to get to 2000 words. With this technique of choosing a modest goal, the idea isn't to simply stop when you reach 500 words, instead, if you have the energy, keep going! On the other hand, if you are exhausted by the time you reach 500 words, feel free to end your writing session.

Some days you will feel awful, and it will be a struggle to get started. If this is the case, tell yourself, "I just need to write 500 words" and use your initiation discipline to get started. After 15 minutes, you might accidentally find yourself in a flow state and end up having an awesome writing session pumping out 1500 words. If you struggle to initiate the writing session, that doesn't mean you are necessarily going to have a bad day.

The next form of discipline required to write effectively is focus. Many writers will find their attention moving away from the task at hand and onto other things. To avoid this problem, isolate yourself from other people, put your cell phone or other distractions in another room, and try your best to remain on task. Since you are likely writing on your computer, you will probably be tempted to browse the internet. Freedom.to is an effective app which can prevent you from accessing certain websites, apps, or the internet as a whole for set periods of time. This will be very useful for some writers.

Other writers need to use the internet for research while they are working. If this is the case for you, a good idea is to dedicate a single device to the sole purpose of writing and research. If you want to watch videos, play games, or engage in some other kind of recreational internet activity use a different device. By using your writing computer for one purpose only it becomes associated with writing in your subconscious, you won't be nearly as likely to get distracted watching videos on youtube.

The final form of discipline which is critical for writers is tolerance for boredom. Some days writing is a blast; you will love typing out your ideas and won't be bored at all. Other days writing is tedious, and you will be thrilled to meet your daily word count.

You can't eliminate boredom from any activity, but you can minimize it by taking advantage of a psychological state called flow. Flow is investigated much more thoroughly in the section on tolerance for boredom; here, we will consider flow in so far as it relates to writing and other creative pursuits. When you are writing, and the words seem to come out effortlessly as if they are being dictated to you by some force outside of yourself, you know that you are in flow. It doesn't feel like you have to work to get the writing onto the page; instead, the ideas freely come out of you. In a state of flow, you not only feel your best, but also the quality of your work is at its highest. This is the optimal state which you ought to encourage to the best of your ability. Flow is the cure for boredom, in a state of flow you are completely engaged and interested.

You can't force yourself to enter flow, but you can engineer an environment more conducive to flow. As mentioned earlier, eliminate distractions to the best of your ability and simply get started; both of these will increase your likelihood of entering into a flow state. Additionally, in order to maximize your chances of entering into a flow state, take deep breaths into your lower abdomen, drink plenty of water, and avoid heavy meals. Many writers are best able to enter flow very early in the morning before eating breakfast.

The following writing program is simple, but that doesn't make it easy. If your writing requires research, you will want to modify the program to include that. Additionally, if you have a lot of commitments, you might want to reduce the requirements of those commitments. On the other hand, if you are an experienced writer with a lot of free time, you can consider increasing the word count goals beyond what is listed.

Weeks 1-2:

Set a specific time and place for writing and stick with it throughout the program. Ideally very early in the morning or late at night and make sure that you are writing in a quiet, isolated place. For the first 2 weeks, write a minimum of 350 words per day.

Weeks 3-4:

For weeks 3 and 4 add an additional 250 words per day, reaching a total of 600 words per day.

Weeks 5-6:

For weeks 5 and 6 add an additional 200 words per day, reaching a total of 800 words per day.

Weeks 7-8:

For weeks 7 and 8 add an additional 200 words per day, reaching a total of 1000 words per day.

Post:

Once you have developed the habit of writing a minimum of 1000 words every single day, you will quickly become a prolific writer. To put this in perspective, 60 000 words is the typical length for an entire book. Considering that some days you will be writing more than 1000 words you will be able to write the first draft of a 60 000 word book in less than 2 months. This might seem like an unachievable goal, but this program should allow most writers to work up to that productivity level within 8 weeks.

HEALTHY EATING IMPROVEMENT PROGRAM

Professional dieticians and health experts disagree on some of the most fundamental questions in terms of what is healthy and whether or not healthy/unhealthy food even exists. To avoid the rabbit hole of dietary science, we will refrain from making any specific recommendations in terms of what you should or shouldn't eat. For the sake of this program, we will assume that you know what foods you should eat and what foods you should avoid for your body and your specific goals.

The following program is very conservative. Some people are able to completely transform their diet overnight and as a result, change the trajectory of their life. However, the evidence suggests that the majority of people who make drastic dietary change end up reverting back to their old ways within a few years and in some cases the rebound is even worse than the original diet. For this reason, it is better for you to gradually improve your dietary habits over the course of months. It is much more efficient to make slow, steady progress than it is to overreach and not make any progress at all.

Note: Before taking on any dietary protocol, you should seek advice from a medical professional.

Weeks 1-2:

Add or replace a healthy meal every single day. During this meal don't eat anything which you shouldn't be eating, for example: don't add too much salt and don't add too much sugar. Make sure to hit and not surpass your caloric/macronutrient requirements if that is relevant.

Weeks 3-4:

Cut out one unhealthy habit from your daily routine. For example, stop adding sugar to your oatmeal or your coffee. Another example would be to refrain from drinking beer after you get home from work.

Weeks 5-6:

Add an additional healthy meal every single day. Follow the same rules that were specified for weeks 1-2.

Week 7-8:

Cut out an additional unhealthy habit from your daily routine.

Post:

Some people will immediately feel better after following this routine; others won't notice much of a difference. However, when it comes to diet, what's important isn't following a healthy plan for 8 weeks; instead you should aim to follow a healthy plan for years on end. This program will help you develop a set of habits which you can maintain for decades, making a permanent impact on your health. If your current diet is very bad and needs a complete makeover you can repeat this program or do a shortened version of it to make further changes as necessary.

General Intermediate Discipline

Pre-requisites: The following plan is for someone who has already acquired a well-established meditation habit, a consistent workout routine, above-average performance at work or in business, and self-educates regularly. Additionally, you shouldn't have any major addiction you have still been unable to overcome. Beyond that, recognize that this program is demanding and shouldn't be attempted during a tumultuous period in your life. Also, this program is not recommended for busy people. Yes, you can certainly pull it off while working a full-time job, but this program isn't a good idea for someone in their first couple of years in BigLaw.

Depending on your commitments you may feel that you don't have enough time to complete the daily objectives. If this is the case, the answer is simple, find time or sleep less. Sleep is important for health and cognitive function, but this is only an 8 week program, you will recover afterwards. Stick with this program all the way to the end and you will experience dramatic improvements in your ability to overcome discomfort, and as a result, your discipline will reach new epic proportions.

The General Intermediate Training Program has two primary elements. The spiritual and the physical. In the beginning, you will eliminate a lot of negative and distracting external inputs from entering into your mind. Additionally, you will dramatically improve your meditation process. Physically you will purify the food and various substances which go into your body. Also, you will enhance your discipline and improve your connection to your body with a very demanding exercise routine based on your specific goals.

It makes sense to detail a general discipline program for intermediates. However, intermediate and advanced training programs for specific aspects of discipline ought to be individualized. If you want to follow an intermediate or advanced program designed to improve any specific trait or aspect of discipline it makes more sense for you to design that program yourself or to find an expert who can design it for you. That being said, because this program is so general, it can apply to anyone who meets the prerequisites and has the available free time.

Note: If you don't work or only work part-time, you should dramatically increase the time spent meditating. Part-time workers should meditate two times as much as is specified in the program and people who don't work and don't own a business at all should meditate three times as much. There is no need to modify the other recommendations, particularly the exercise routine because further increases in intensity could cause some physical problems.

Weeks 1-2:

Eliminate all unnecessary social media use, cell phone applications, and digital entertainment. This includes but is not limited to television, pornography, Netflix, Youtube, Instagram, Facebook, etc.

Start waking up before sunrise every day. Set a specific time and stick with it throughout the program. Note: if you have to stay up late for some important commitments you can skip this specific step. However, you may need to find creative ways to get more free time out of your schedule.

Also, increase your daily meditation to 30 minutes every day and do it first thing upon waking.

Weeks 3-4:

Eliminate any unhealthy food, alcohol, and unnecessary drugs from your routine. This includes cigarettes and legal opiates. Quit cold turkey unless this would endanger your health.

Increase the intensity of your workout routine. Since having an exercise routine is a prerequisite, everyone doing this program will be following a different routine with different goals.

If you currently practice yoga 4 times per week increase that number to 7. If you are a bodybuilder increase the number of sets, you perform and emphasize difficult compound exercises for the lower body. If you are a runner, add in a session during your lunch break. If you practice martial arts add some kata or other exercises after your meditation every morning.

Weeks 5-6:

Meditate for an additional hour every single day. This can be done for multiple sessions or in a single hour-long session.

Weeks 7-8:

At this point, you should have adapted to more intense physical training. Increase the intensity of your exercise routine even further. The yogi who was practicing 7 times per week should increase to 10 sessions. The bodybuilder will have mostly adapted to his higher volume routine and will be able to push the volume even further. The runner can add in 3 additional runs per week.

At this point, the intensity of your physical routine should be extremely demanding. You will likely get comments from other people saying that you are doing too much. You will also likely experience a decrease in your performance. Don't worry; you are only going to maintain this level for two weeks. After the program is over, you will feel better again.

Post:

Once you have completed the program, you should reduce the intensity of your physical routine substantially. First, you should go back to doing whatever you were doing before the program started for 1 or 2 weeks until you feel normal. Then you can increase the intensity if you want, but don't go as far as you did during weeks 7 and 8.

In addition to tremendous gains in your discipline, you will likely have experienced massive improvements in your understanding of the meditative process. Your clarity of mind will be at a new unprecedented level.

While your physical performance may have temporarily gone down, you will have learned more about what your body is capable of. After resting for a couple of weeks, you will likely notice a rebound and your performance will probably reach new impressive heights you never managed before the program.

Other habits in this program can be maintained if you feel that they benefit your life. By the end of the program, you will be meditating for more than an hour and a half every day. This will be highly beneficial for your mental state if you keep it up; however, 90 minutes a day will eat up a lot of your time needed for other things and may not be worth it for many people.

Certainly you can keep waking up before the sun rises, eating healthy, avoiding recreational drugs, and limiting social/digital media usage. Maintaining these aspects of the program will improve most people's lives.

Sample Advanced Discipline Program

The following advanced discipline program is not suitable for everyone. Not only do you need a very strong foundation to attempt this program, but your own advanced discipline program may need to be more individualized. However, you could design your own advanced discipline program and model it after this one.

Prerequisites: Lots of experience sticking with plans, tremendous medium-distance discipline. An intensive exercise routine which you have maintained for years without skipping a single session. A daily meditative program which you never miss no matter what. Daily self-education and a very healthy lifestyle overall. Completed the general intermediate discipline program without missing a single day.

The general intermediate discipline training program is notably focused on the physical (diet, drugs, exercise) and the spiritual (meditation, digital/social media). This specific advanced discipline program is focused on developing your cerebral abilities, knowledge, and your vocation, however, you could design an advanced discipline program with different goals.

This program is 12 weeks long and is very intensive. At certain points, you may feel like skipping some of the habits you worked so hard to develop in the past, but you should maintain them no matter what. In a worst-case scenario where you have to decide between maintaining your cornerstone habits like meditation or quitting this advanced training program early, choose to quit this advanced training program.

To prevent yourself from getting into a situation where you might need to quit you are recommended to put the other aspects of your life on maintenance mode throughout the course of this program. For example, if you normally workout six days per week, cut it down to three days per week to maintain. Or if you normally meditate for 30 minutes per day, cut it down to 15 minutes per day to maintain.

If you are ready for this advanced discipline program, you probably have a lot going on in your life and are fairly busy. Try to find a way to cut your commitments down to a minimum level throughout the course of the program. However, don't jeopardize the other aspects of your life. If you are too busy to do this program right now, wait for as long as necessary until you are ready.

Absolutely do not attempt this program if you have any major obligations or goals which will eat up a lot of your free time.

This program is designed for someone who wants to either improve their business or improve their performance at work. If you don't own a business and aren't interested in improving your performance at work use the time which is supposed to be dedicated to that goal as additional time for learning difficult things or alternatively try working on a big creative project such as writing a book.

Also, because the demands of this program are so high, there will be a tendency to slack off in terms of focus or intensity. There is no point in showing up for work early if you aren't going to get a lot of work done.

While you are learning and while you are working, keep the intensity high and try your absolute best to stay on task the whole time. Yes there will be moments and even entire days when you aren't performing your best, keep at it, try your best, and your ability to focus will return eventually.

Note: If you already work for 10 hours or more per day, the specific recommendations of this program won't fit into your schedule. Feel free to cut the amount of added time substantially to meet the needs of your particular situation.

Weeks 1-2:

Show up for your job 30 minutes earlier and stay 30 minutes later every day or if you own a business, increase your workday by an additional hour every day. If you can't show up early for work, study something which will make you better at your job for an hour per workday.

Start waking up at 4:30am. Skip this step if you have commitments which require you to stay up late at night. If you can't wake up at 4:30 am for some reason, you will need to find other creative ways to squeeze extra time out of your schedule.

Weeks 3-4:

Read something difficult or learn something difficult for 45 minutes every single day. This could include math, physics, biology, chemistry, learning a new language, or computer programming. You can choose something which will make you better at your job or something which will benefit you in some other way over the long run. Alternatively, you can use this time to work on online courses.

Weeks 5-6:

Show up for work an additional 30 minutes earlier and stay at work for an additional 30 minutes every single day. At this point, you will be arriving at work an hour earlier and staying for an hour later than you did at the beginning of the program. If you are unable to enter your workplace that early spend 1 hour per day studying something which will make you better at your job. If you run your own business work for an additional hour per day on your business.

Weeks 7-8:

Self-educate for an additional hour per day. By now you will be learning for at least one hour and 45 minutes per day. You can do this all in one session or in parts.

Weeks 9-10:

Show up for work an additional 45 minutes earlier and stay an additional 45 minutes later. In total, you will be arriving at work an hour and 45 minutes earlier and staying for an hour and 45 minutes later than you did at the beginning of the program. If you are unable to enter your workplace that early spend an hour and a half per day studying something that will make you better at your job. If you run your own business work for an additional hour and a half per day on your business.

Weeks 11-12:

Self-educate for an additional hour per day. At this point, you will be learning for at least 2 hours and 45 minutes per day. You can do this in one session or in parts.

If you add together the additional time you will be spending working and the amount of time you will be self-educating, by weeks 11-12 you will be occupied for 6 hours and 15 minutes more than you were at the beginning of the program. This will be very intensive; however it is appropriate for an advanced program.

Post:

By the end of this program, you will likely be exhausted. You should cut down to whatever you were doing in terms of self-education and your work before the start of the program and maintain this reduced load for 2 weeks. Afterwards you can ramp back up to a higher level.

By the end of this program, you will have made a substantial amount of progress with either your business or your work. Also, you will have dramatically improved your concentration ability as well as developed skills and knowledge, which are normally difficult to learn.

Additionally, since the time demands of this program are so high, you will have gotten better at squeezing every last minute out of your day. You will realize how many more opportunities there are to get things done.

9. When Discipline is About to Crack

Often the main difference between someone who is able to improve their discipline over the long run and someone who isn't, comes down to their ability to hold the line when they are about to give in. How do you know if your discipline is about to crack? Any time you are close to breaking a promise that you made to yourself. The one exception where it is ok to break a promise you made to yourself is if following through involves a realistic possibility of causing serious damage to yourself or other people. This includes physical injury or financial harm.

Interspersed throughout this book are various recommendations for saving you at the last moment when you feel like you don't have any discipline left. This specific chapter highlights additional valuable techniques.

Remember your Second Wind

Long-distance runners know that if they keep pushing past the point where they feel like giving up, they will get a huge boost of energy which allows them to run faster and seemingly use less energy. The scientific explanation behind the second wind has yet to be determined. Some researchers use physiological explanations, and others claim that it is purely psychological. Whatever the case, the second wind exists, and it is useful.

The second wind is also important when it comes to nonphysical activities involving discipline. If you are able to push through the feeling that you want to quit, you will experience a resurgence of discipline. Sometimes just remembering that the second wind exists is enough to push you to the next level. If you are thinking about giving up, remind yourself that if you can keep going past the uncomfortable period, eventually you will be rewarded with a boost of energy.

Each Step Forward makes you Stronger

Completing the task and meeting the commitment is just the surface goal. The deeper more important goal is actually to acquire more discipline in the process. Ideally, acquiring more discipline should be the deeper motivation behind all of the decisions that you make. Sometimes, when you are about to give in, all it takes to get back on track is a reminder that making the right decision will make you stronger and making the wrong decision will make you weaker. Imagine you run a business and have a goal of making 10 cold calls by the end of the afternoon, but you are feeling overwhelmed and feel like giving up at 5. Remind yourself that powering through the discomfort and completing all 10 calls will make you mentally stronger and will improve your skills when it comes to cold calling. On the other hand, giving in to discomfort will reduce your mental strength and neglect an opportunity to perfect your craft.

Make it about Someone Else

Usually, the challenging things we attempt to accomplish not only benefit us, but they also benefit other people as well. For example, when you perform well at work, it not only improves your individual professional situation, but it also improves your company as a whole benefitting your coworkers and your clients. Additionally, improving your performance at work increases your job security and your long-term career prospects, which is ultimately good for your family.

Another example is a physical training partner. When you show up to the gym and give it your all, focus hard at the dojo, or push yourself on your morning run, your training partner is more likely to reach their goals. If you are feeling weak, stop thinking about yourself, start thinking about all the other people who depend on you.

Here is a scenario which illustrates this idea. You are climbing a physically demanding mountain with a group of experienced mountaineers. This mountain is the tallest and most challenging climb any of you have attempted. As the days go by you find yourself feeling more and more exhausted, you know that you have the physical resources to make it to the top, but you aren't sure if you have the drive. Every step is a challenge, and your mind continuously reinforces the fact that you still have a day and a half of climbing before reaching the peak. Negative thoughts and a desire to quit fester in your mind.

However, you know that this climb will be difficult for everyone, and surely your teammates are struggling as well. Start focusing on them. Stop worrying if you can make it to the top, instead, make it your mission to ensure that your entire team makes it to the top.

Improve the moral of everyone, make jokes, and don't let anyone know how exhausted you really are (unless you are in physical danger). Figure out who is struggling the most and encourage them. What you will find is that by diverting your mental energy away from yourself and onto other people you won't feel tired anymore. You will escape the negative feedback loops in your mind and access the deep energy resources hidden inside of you.

Remind yourself of the Difficult things you have already Overcome

No matter how old you are or how long you have been on the disciplined path, you will have already had to overcome numerous challenges in your life. These may have been challenges you chose to take on yourself. For example, climbing a large mountain. On the other hand, there may have been challenges put in front of you. For example, the loss of a loved one or an unexpected financial hardship. Whether you chose to take on these challenges yourself or if they were unavoidable inconveniences of life, you can always use these experiences as fuel for your discipline.

You might not feel like going for your daily swim, but if you think back to the time you swam 4 kilometers without stopping, your daily 1-kilometer swim won't seem like much. If you are working a challenging contract, and are having trouble keeping your discipline together, think back to the times when you had to overcome similar or even more difficult situations.

Challenging experiences can make you stronger, but they can also make you weaker, it all depends on how you respond. Sometimes we have a difficult experience, and it traumatizes us because it was either too intense or we simply didn't have the cognitive/emotional tools to deal with the event.

If you apply the technique of using past challenges to your advantage, you are more likely to respond in a positive way to negative events. By learning to use your negative experiences, you become more emotionally and psychologically resilient

USE A BUDDY SYSTEM

A critical part of the term self-discipline is the word "self," ultimately, you have to rely on yourself in your discipline journey. That being said, recruiting the help of someone else to keep you accountable can be a useful aid, particularly if you are struggling to keep it together on your own. Ideally, your discipline buddy will also be on a similar quest to become as disciplined as possible. Unfortunately, there aren't many people out there with this specific goal. If it isn't possible to find someone who is trying to become more disciplined find someone who is also pursuing self-development or at least someone who genuinely wants the best for you.

There are different ways you can organize the buddy arrangement. The simplest system is to report daily to your buddy on whether or not you followed through with your commitments. There doesn't have to be any punishments, rewards, or any other information shared.

Some people using the buddy system prefer to have some kind of stakes to make sure that they actually follow through. For example, you could give your buddy $100, and if you fail to meet your commitments, they will donate that money to a political cause you detest.

The buddy system is very effective for some people, but unnecessary for others. If you are having trouble sticking to your commitments without reporting to someone else there is probably some kind of weakness in your discipline which you need to address, however, in the meantime, having a discipline buddy will keep you accountable.

BECOME INSPIRED BY THE CHALLENGE ITSELF

You can look at how much you have already done in pursuit of your current goal and become inspired by that. If you are training to climb a huge mountain and have been sticking to your routine for a month and a half, use that fact to push you past the point of giving up. Use the very fact that you are attempting such an impressive mountain as motivation. You can say to yourself "who else could have made it this far?" or "How crazy am I to take on such a big challenge".

If you are about to give in during training, remind yourself of how challenging the experience will be once you are on the actual mountain. Remind yourself that if you slack off in training, the actual climb will be much more painful and you might not even make it to the top.

Use the Enemy Metaphor

Create an enemy, real or imaginary, who is just as motivated and focused as you are to succeed. Imagine them getting up early in the morning and putting in work in an attempt to defeat you.

If you do choose to use a real person as your "enemy" remember that the goal isn't to defeat or humiliate them; instead the goal is to use them as a motivating force. Most of the time you shouldn't even tell them that they are "the enemy." Just pursue your goals, stick to the plan, and if you feel like giving in, remind yourself of how hard "the enemy" is working.

If you create an imaginary enemy, make them as cartoonish and threatening as possible. Use disturbing and symbolic imagery; you want to create an emotional reaction within yourself.

If you are struggling to implement a gym routine picture a maniac who is also in the gym every day trying to get in better shape than you, so they hurt you or someone you love. Feel free to get graphic if that helps.

If you are a programmer and you are struggling to get to work, imagine another programmer who is awake in the middle of the night drinking energy drinks fanatically writing code trying to take away your customers.

If this idea of using "the enemy" as motivation disturbs you or makes you cringe remember that you don't have to use the enemy every day or even every week. Make use of the enemy only when it is necessary to get past the hurdle of giving in.

The 40 Percent Rule

David Goggins' story was described in more detail earlier in this book. As a quick reminder, he is an ultramarathon runner, a former navy seal, and former pull-up world-record holder. Not only did Goggins lose more than 100 pounds in less than 3 months to meet Navy Seals requirements, but he also survived three hell weeks in navy seal training, ran 100 miles without practice despite weighing 260 lbs, and completed his third navy seal training with two broken legs running upwards of 30 miles a week. Through his various unbelievable feats of mental toughness, Goggins made a simple but extremely powerful discovery about the human mind.

Most people give up at 40% of their capacity

"Most" isn't referring to your average couch potato, by "most" Goggins is including very disciplined highly functional people. The truth is that hardly anyone even comes close to their full potential. According to Goggins, our mind plays a trick on us. It convinces us that we are approaching our limit in terms of pain and other forms of discomfort. But, if you are capable of pushing through these false signals, you will find a well of energy within yourself you had no idea existed.

When you are about to give up this means that you are probably at around 40 percent of your actual capacity. If you don't believe it's true, test it for yourself, see how far you can go.

BE GRATEFUL

Everyone has something to be grateful for. What are you grateful for? Your job? Your family? Your health? The country you live in?

Sometimes when you push your discipline, your identity or another subsystem resists and tries to weaken you by creating an emotionally disturbing environment in your mind. Gratefulness is a useful tool to get you out of dark places.

If you have been overweight your entire life and are starting to eat healthier your identity will likely try to sabotage you. At first, it will not interfere with your new plan to eat more vegetables and less sweets; it doesn't want to battle motivation directly. But, after your motivation has subsided, your identity will launch an assault. It will start to say things like "you are fat, and there is nothing you can do about it" or "don't try to resist the ice cream, you know that you will give in eventually". The identity is clever, and it will know exactly what it needs to say and when it needs to say it.

When you are in that dark place and feel like you are about to give in to the identity's attacks, this is the time to be grateful. Think about how lucky you for all the great things and people in your life. Be grateful for the fact that you have managed to make it this far. Be grateful for discipline itself. Discipline is what gives us the ability to accomplish and pursue so many wonderful things. Discipline is the force that allows you to overcome the manipulative nature of your identity.

By being grateful, you will stop your identity in its tracks and take yourself out of that dark state of mind your identity tried to trap in you. If you can defeat your identity when you are at your weakest, you will gain free reign when you are strong.

Perhaps your identity will come back for a second assault. However, if you last long enough with your new lifestyle, your identity will realize that it needs to accept your change and adapt to the new version of you.

You are still Breathing

An extension of gratefulness, This is the last line of defence when nothing else is working. Remember that if you are still breathing, you still have some willpower left in you.

Despite the commonly touted metaphor that willpower is a muscle and that it gets depleted, as long as you are breathing, you still have the capacity to overcome the weakness inside of yourself. Discipline may get depleted partially, but it is never depleted entirely.

Be grateful for the fact that you can still breathe and therefore, can still make difficult choices. No matter what your identity tells you, no matter how awful you feel, you always have the ability to make the disciplined choice.

Breath is a powerful tool. At your darkest moment, remember to breathe. Instead of breathing into your upper chest, take slow deep breaths through your nose into your lower abdomen. Feel your mood elevate as oxygen replenishes your discipline stores.

Never feel like you have to give in. It doesn't matter how tired you are, how much pain you feel or how much you want to give up, as long as you are breathing, you can still push forward.

10. Evaluating different Discipline Techniques

Due to the recent increase in interest in discipline and personal development as a whole, a number of different techniques for increasing discipline and motivation have gained popularity.

Some of these techniques are more effective than others. Meditation has existed for thousands of years, and it is one of the most effective things you can do for your self-discipline and self-knowledge. On the other hand, even the least effective techniques at least have the benefit of the placebo effect.

This chapter will be an assessment of some of the most popular things that people are doing to improve their habits, productivity, motivation, and self-discipline. We will not only be considering the effectiveness of the protocol, but also which aspects of discipline are improved if any, and finally deciding whether or not there are any negative side effects.

Daily Cold Showers

A James Bond favorite, the benefits of cold water therapy have been touted for centuries. Recently, cold showers have gained popularity in certain personal development communities. The recent popularity likely originated from Tim Ferriss's glowing recommendation in his book *The Four Hour Body*.

While a discussion on the potential health benefits of cold showers are outside the scope of this book, there is good reason to believe that they will enhance your journey to improve your discipline.

Cold showers will energize you and increase your overall awareness. They are particularly effective for people who are lacking in energy. Most people feel great and ready to take on the day after drying off. Additionally, daily cold showers will exercise your discipline by forcing you to do something you don't want to do every single day.

There are a couple of different ways you can have a cold shower.

Contrast therapy is a popular option; in doing this, you go back and forth between hot and cold water. A Scottish shower, James Bond's preferred style, is a type of contrast therapy. To do this, you start off with warm water and go through the normal cleaning process. Once you have finished cleaning yourself, you gradually reduce the water temperature until it is at the coldest point. In the beginning, you might struggle to last a few seconds, try to work up to a couple of minutes at least.

The most brutal and discipline-testing way to have a cold shower is by starting at the coldest temperature and never turning it onto warm throughout the whole cleaning process. This can be especially savage in chillier weather when the pipes are cold. You might imagine that contrast therapy is more unpleasant, but something about starting off with warm water makes it easier to manage.

Cold showers exercise and strengthen your initiation discipline because it takes some effort to force yourself to get into the cold water every day. This is particularly true when you go directly into the cold water without the warm water at the beginning. Cold showers also strengthen pain tolerance and your courage/vulnerability to a lesser extent.

There are a few potential downsides to cold water therapy. If you are extremely stressed in a frantic ungrounded sort of way cold showers could potentially push you over the edge in terms of overall arousal. Also, cold showers require a lot of discipline and take a long time to get used to. If it normally takes you a couple of weeks to develop a habit, it may take you months or even a year to get used to cold showers. They could possibly use up some of your extra discipline which might be better served taking on new habits.

INTERMITTENT FASTING

Just like cold water therapy, people have been fasting for a very long time. Intermittent fasting has recently gained popularity because of its ability to increase mental energy benefits, help with weight loss, and supposedly improve overall health.

Intermittent fasting, unlike other forms of fasting, occurs on a daily basis. People following this dietary practice are only allowed to eat during fixed eating windows throughout the day. The length and time of these eating windows depend on the person.

Probably the most common recommendation is to eat during an eight-hour eating window, for example, between 1 pm - 9 pm and then not consuming any calories for the rest of the day and night. Other people will eat during a 12-hour eating window and some people will go as far as to limit themselves to eating a maximum of 1 meal per day without snacking.

First off, intermittent fasting can absolutely contribute to weight loss. Not through it's supposed effect on hormonal levels, but rather because it makes it a lot easier to sustain a caloric deficit for most people. However, you can certainly overeat while intermittent fasting and fail to lose weight or in some cases even gain weight. Whether or not you are intermittent fasting, if you want to lose weight, it is best to eat foods which are relatively filling compared to their caloric content, e.g. legumes, steel-cut oats, brown rice, lean meats, fish, vegetables, etc. If you really want to lose weight and nothing else is working, you have to count calories.

This isn't a diet book, so we will return to the more pressing concern. How does intermittent fasting affect discipline?

Many people experience substantial discomfort and a lot of hunger when they first start fasting. But most people adapt to the new eating schedule within a few weeks.

Experiences intermittent fasting vary, but increased energy and focus throughout the fasting period is very common. Additionally, the sheer act of overcoming your hunger will exercise your discipline and boost your confidence.

Another benefit is that you aren't distracted by the need to eat throughout the entire fasting period. If you are a writer or do something else which requires extended periods of focus, try intermittent fasting, and you may find that you can work longer and more efficiently than ever before.

Now for the downsides:

1) Intermittent fasting is probably not optimal for physical performance, particularly for people who need to build a lot of muscle mass.

2) Just like cold water therapy, intermittent fasting can increase overall stress on your system. So if you are stressed out in a frantic, scattered way, you might experience more problems intermittent fasting. Additionally, people with extreme anxiety are recommended to eat a big breakfast with plenty of protein and fat, intermittent fasting, on the other hand, could possibly exacerbate anxiety symptoms.

3) Many people binge when they are finally allowed to eat and as a result, lose a lot of their energy and concentration levels. Additionally, this can cause weight gain and gastrointestinal problems. Intermittent fasting is not an excuse to eat too much, eat unhealthy foods, or drink excessive amounts of alcohol.

4) The following isn't a serious problem, but it is a gentle warning for people who love coffee. Many people who follow intermittent fasting develop a serious caffeine addiction drinking copious amounts of black coffee during their fast. Caffeine helps suppress appetite, and it can feel nice to taste something bitter when you are hungry. If you love coffee and you are going to try intermittent fasting, it is a good idea to buy a lot of decaf coffee ahead of time. Note: Some fasting purists believe that you lose the health benefits of

intermittent fasting if you consume anything other than pure water during your fast.

Although it doesn't work well for everyone, intermittent fasting is absolutely worth trying out. Following an 8 hour fast is a good place to start, stick with it for at least two weeks and be ready for a massive productivity boost.

Waking up Extremely Early

Former navy seal commander Jocko Willink has recently helped popularize the habit of waking up at 4:30 am every single day of the week. If you are able to structure it in your life, this is a very powerful behavioural change.

If you work a job with normal hours or if you have other things which distract you during the day, waking up extremely early will give you the time you need to get things done.

For example, let's say you need to leave for work at 8 am, here is how your morning could look.

4:30 am: Wake up, meditate, turn off your alarm, put on your workout clothes which you prepared for yourself last night, brush your teeth, and walk into your home office.

5 am: Get in 75 minutes of uninterrupted work on whatever project you are currently focusing on. This is a great time to study difficult concepts, write, create any kind of art, compose music, or edit video.

6:15 am: Hit the home gym for a 1 hour workout session. You are already wearing your workout clothes.

7:15 am: Take a 5-minute shower, put on your work clothes which you already laid out for yourself the night before, do anything else that needs to be done, and be out of the house by 8 am.

In the above example, you have already made serious progress on an important project and got in a decent amount of exercise before you even left for work. You might notice that there is no downtime in the above schedule; you simply efficiently go from task to task. This is much easier to do when you wake up extremely early; you will likely feel more productive and have fewer distractions. Also, you will probably find that you can concentrate more easily on challenging mental tasks.

You can modify the above schedule anyway you want to fit your lifestyle. You can get up earlier or later, there is nothing magical about 4:30 am. Jocko Willink is very busy during the day with multiple businesses and other time-consuming projects, so he likes to workout first thing in the morning, other people find that they have time to workout later in the day and prefer to focus on their creative projects as soon as they get up.

Whatever the case for you, put your most important tasks in between waking up and leaving for work, particularly things which you might otherwise not have time to do.

Jocko Willink and many others who wake up extremely early like to fast in the morning as well. This is worth trying because it will give you even more free time. You will notice in the example above there is no scheduled time for breakfast.

Waking up extremely early will stress your discipline because it doesn't feel good to get up out of bed so early. But, once you are out of bed and moving, you will start to feel a lot better.

There are some pretty straightforward downsides to getting up extremely early.

1) It can result in you being sleep deprived. Some people need more sleep than others. Jocko Willink openly admits that he has slept less than the average person for his entire life and that this has been exacerbated since going to war. He often wakes up in the middle of the night thinking about his experiences in combat. The solution is simple, go to bed earlier. However, the following will explain why going to bed earlier can be a problem as well.

2) Let's say you need 8 hours of sleep per night. This means that if you get up at 4:30 am, you need to be in bed with the lights off by 8:30 pm at the latest. This will severely limit your social life and other activities which you do at night. Most people need some time to get ready for bed as well. Suppose you are out with friends and it will take you about 30 minutes to get home, you also know that you need 45 minutes to get ready for bed when you actually get home. This means that you need to leave by 7:15 pm at the latest in order to get your full 8 hours of sleep. If you only need 6 hours of sleep per night, you would need to leave by 9:15 pm, which is still early, but it isn't unreasonable.

Waking up extremely early works for people who either don't have evening activities, don't need much sleep, or choose to sacrifice sleep on certain nights when they have interesting engagements in the evening.

Note: Jocko Willink certainly isn't the only productive person who gets up extremely early; however, his approach is an excellent model.

ORDERLY HABITS

Immanuel Kant was one of the greatest and most influential philosophers of all time. Despite publishing his most important works in the 18th century, Kant's ideas are still important in the modern-day. The quality of Kant's ideas and his productivity are likely attributable to his legendary daily routine which he strictly adhered to for more than 40 years.

Kant would wake up at 5 am, drink tea, smoke his pipe and meditate. From there he would write and prepare his lectures. Between 7 am to 11 am he would teach at the local University in Konigsberg Prussia. After finishing his lectures, he would write until lunch where he would eat at exactly the same restaurant every single day. Next, he would leave for a walk on the same route at exactly 3:30 pm, supposedly people were known to set their clocks based on this walk. After his walk he would spend the evening chatting with his best friend and then return home where he would read or do some light work and then go to bed at exactly 10pm every single night.

There are varying reports on Kant's exact routine and his life, including some slight variances on the above schedule. Also, there are reports that Kant never traveled more than sixteen kilometers out his hometown of Konigsberg, Prussia, but other people say that this isn't true. Ultimately, the exact details of Kant's life and daily routine aren't important; what is undeniable is that he was extremely orderly in his lifestyle. The relevant question to this book is whether or not orderliness enhance your discipline and the quality of your life overall.

The Big Five Personality Inventory is widely recognized among psychologists as the best measure of personality in existence. While it is impossible to fully measure someone's personality using a written test, the Big Five Inventory is the closest thing we have to actually doing this. As you may already know, the Big Five Personality Inventory includes five traits. One of the five traits, conscientious, encompasses orderliness in addition to other qualities. It is characterized by the following qualities.

- Productivity
- Efficiency
- Reliability
- Attention to detail
- Responsibility
- Organization
- Cleanliness

Understandmyself.com is a website run by a group of psychology PhDs which breaks down each of the Big Five traits into two distinct but related aspects. Conscientious splits into orderliness and industriousness. Industriousness has to do with your drive to get things done and be efficient. Orderliness is your tendency to follow a routine, be neat, and stay on task. These sub-traits are distinct but correlated to each other.

The ideal amount of orderliness in your life will depend in part on your natural orderliness level.

If you are someone who prefers flexibility, spontaneity, and doesn't mind chaos or unpredictability, go ahead and keep your schedule somewhat open. However, when it comes to discipline, generally speaking, the more orderliness you can tolerate, the better. If you have lower than average orderliness, try adding some routines into your life. You will likely see a productivity boost. Keep pushing your orderliness until you reach your limit. You will know that you are at your limit when you struggle to stick to your schedule and you feel some existential hopelessness.

When you reach your limit back off and add some flexibility into your routine until you start to feel comfortable again. After a couple of months, try making your routine more orderly again and see how you feel. Over time you should be able to tolerate more and more orderliness.

Strict daily routines are certainly not necessary for productivity; however they can be very beneficial for a couple of different reasons.

1) Daily routines mean that you don't have to waste energy making decisions throughout the day. If you always go to the gym at 7 pm, you don't have to use up any time or mental resources deciding if and when you go to the gym.

2) Daily routines help you develop momentum throughout the day. Something which is seemingly trivial like making the bed in the morning can help you get on the right track to continue making disciplined decisions. A strict daily routine with a number of different

habits which you have maintained over a long period of time can give you a nearly unstoppable discipline.

DIGITAL MINIMALISM AND SOCIAL MEDIA

Cal Newport, a professor of computer science at Georgetown University, recently published *Digital Minimalism* a guide and call to action for a world where social media and the internet, in general, is taking up more and more of our time and mental energy. In this book, Dr. Newport explains a lot of the problems that social media is causing and then provides a solution. He recommends quitting all unnecessary social media and internet-based activities for a month. You are allowed to continue checking your email (or other things) if that is necessary for your work; however you ought to keep it to a minimum.

After this month away from most internet-based activities, you are meant to reevaluate everything you used to do online. First, decide whether each particular application or website is worth returning to. If yes, create a plan to get the most benefit from that application or website with minimal distraction or other downsides.

There are other ways people are introducing digital minimalism into their lives. For example, as mentioned earlier in this book, a good idea is to delete the application from your phone and only login through a web browser. You might worry that disconnecting from social media will damage your interpersonal relationships. Normally, this isn't the case. More likely, it will improve your relationships because you will have more time and energy for face-to-face connections.

Overall digital minimalism is highly recommended. Cal Newport's month-long digital declutter is absolutely worth trying.

Relaxation Habits

Many professional athletes use ice baths, deep tissue massage, and other techniques to improve their recovery. Since discipline partially operates like a muscle, it makes sense to consider employing special relaxation habits as well.

Some professional athletes don't use any recovery techniques at all; in fact, some barely even regulate their diet and sleep. This is analogous to the way that many people do whatever they feel like doing during their relaxation time.

The question is, are certain activities going to rest your discipline more efficiently than other activities?

There are a lot of different ways people like to unwind, this includes watching television or movies, playing video games, using social media, chatting with people online, browsing youtube, chatting with friends or family in person, exercising, going for long walks, reading, meditating, taking a nap, going into nature, driving, listening to podcasts, eating, going to the bar, reading or watching the news, and much more. All of the above activities can potentially help you restore your discipline. Often personal development writers will suggest not playing video games, using social media, learning about politics, or other high-intensity activities in order to unwind because these activities can actually increase your stress.

While they might increase your stress, this is part of the idea. They help you escape from all the activities you performed earlier in the day, which stressed your discipline. So it's not necessarily a bad idea to debate politics after a long day at work. There is nothing wrong with including some stressful activities in your unwinding process.

That being said, there are certain activities which are extremely effective for unwinding. These include: long walks without a cell phone, exercising, going into nature, chatting with friends or family, and meditation. Depending on the length of your unwinding process, consider adding one or two of the above recommendations to your evening routine and testing to see how you feel the next day. Chances are that you will be more rested and more capable of taking on challenges than you normally would.

11. THE PITFALLS OF IMPROVING SELF-DISCIPLINE

Discipline is by far the most important virtue. After all, every single other virtue relies on a strong discipline. That being said, in the process of developing any quality or skill, there are certain risks associated with it.

JEALOUSY

As a direct result of becoming more disciplined, your accomplishments will be more impressive. Some of the people around you are likely to feel personally threatened by your success. It's not their higher-self that is threatened; it is their identity. After all, if you are able to do so much, what does this say about them?

When you are close to someone, your identities will make an agreement behind your backs. They will decide to coordinate efforts to make sure that both of you don't change. However, when you are improving your discipline, you will experience some of the greatest changes in your life. If the people close to you are weak and are controlled by their identity, they may lash out at you when they see you becoming a better version of yourself. This might manifest itself in blunt "you have changed" comments, or it may show with more subtle jabs at your newfound success. These sorts of comments or actions are particularly dangerous because their identity isn't the only force trying to hold you back; your identity is trying to do exactly the same thing. Their identity is using whatever methods it can to try to give your identity the fuel it needs to retake control. When you hear these sorts of comments laugh them off. If they make you angry use that as fuel to become more disciplined. If they make you question what you are doing, remember that their comments don't come from genuine concern, but rather they come from a place of insecurity. In some cases, their jealousy will cause them to somehow try to sabotage your success in more sinister ways. For example: a boss or a coworker who tries to prevent you from getting a promotion. Or a friend who attempts to sabotage your marriage.

Because you don't necessarily know who will be offended by your success and who will lash out, it is best to remain humble and downplay your accomplishments whenever possible. Naturally, if you are trying to sell something or are running a business, it is a good idea to talk about what you are doing at every opportunity. But make sure to intersperse your sales pitch with a self-deprecating comment or two. Not everyone is controlled by their identity, in fact, many people will be overjoyed by your new zest for life. They will encourage you, they will push you to the next level, and they will want some of what you have made for yourself. Always remember who celebrates your success; these people should be treasured.

Perfectionism

There is a feedback loop between self-discipline and trying to be the best version of yourself you can possibly be. As your discipline

SELF-DISCIPLINE: THE ART OF BECOMING MORE HUMAN

increases, you will need to seek out new challenges to stretch your abilities; this means that you are constantly looking for ways to improve yourself. In order to continue to stretch your abilities your self-discipline will need to improve in order to compensate. If you can enter into this feedback loop, you will be able to rapidly transform your life. This transformation is generally positive, but the side effects can be a certain amount of neurotic perfectionism.

This book stresses a very general broad idea of discipline, meaning that there are a number of different ways you can improve yourself. Having so many things you can do to make your life better should make you feel optimistic, however, some of the time you may feel overwhelmed by all of the different parts of your life you will eventually need to work on.

People respond to perfectionism in three different ways.

First, some people will try to do everything at once. They will want to improve their fitness, their career, their diet, their courage/vulnerability, their education, and start meditating all at the same time. If you try to do this, you will probably only last for a short period of time before your motivation disappears and you revert to the same habits you had in the beginning or possibly even degenerate below your baseline.

The second typical response to perfectionism is to do nothing at all. You may feel like you will never be able to improve all of these different aspects of your life, so you don't end up improving any of them. This is a form of "paralysis by analysis."

> *"Prioritize and Execute."*
>
> - Jocko Willink, former Navy Seal Commander

Find one or two aspects of your life, which need to be improved, create a plan lasting anywhere from two to twelve weeks, execute your plan. After you have followed through with your program, reevaluate, and create another plan.

Do not feel like everything needs to be improved all at once or even within the next couple of years. Decide what is going to have the biggest impact right now and focus on that. You can move on to the other aspects of your life when it is the right time.

Losing Flexibility

In recent decades the bodybuilding and powerlifting community has learned to embrace the importance of stretching and other mobility-based exercises. Muscle-bound beasts like Kelly Starett have been able to earn a comfortable living teaching lifters how to increase their range of motion. This is in stark contrast to the "17 exercises for giant triceps" approach.

Why are gym rats suddenly so focused on mobility? The answer is actually fairly self-evident. If you move a muscle through a range of motion for years, particularly if it is a partial range of motion, you lose flexibility in that joint over time.

So If you go into the gym and push heavy iron day in and day out without stretching you will become more and more immobile. Bodybuilders don't have to move like ballerinas, but the gradual loss of range of motion from resistance exercises can limit the sorts of exercises which they can perform and in some cases, it can result in pain or injury.

Fortunately, for serious lifters, it turns out that it is actually fairly easy to maintain and improve flexibility by performing certain mobility exercises every day.

Note: the problem is not that the lifters are too strong or too muscular; there are plenty of examples of very strong muscular people who are also totally mobile and healthy. Instead, the joint problems emerge in the process of developing muscularity and strength. This distinction is important when we draw our connection back to discipline.

As has been discussed earlier, discipline has a lot of the same properties as a muscle. And if you use it every single day without stretching, it can become tight and immobile.

There are two implications of this analogy. One of them is literal, and the other is figurative. However, both of these implications are important for someone who is putting in a strong effort into developing their discipline.

The first, more literal implication, is that in the process of becoming disciplined, there is a tendency to become too structured and orderly losing one's ability to adapt in the process. Fortunately, it is possible to become extremely disciplined while maintaining your adaptability at the same time.

One strategy for maintaining adaptability is to dedicate some period of the day to free time. This doesn't have to be purely recreational time; however it shouldn't be dedicated to any particular activity. You could spend this time reading, writing, or working on projects which you normally wouldn't have the time to get around to doing.

Another technique you can use to maintain your flexibility is to push yourself and try to do something which you aren't sure you can actually complete. This will have the added benefit of testing the limits of your discipline. Many people drastically underestimate their capacity for discipline until they actually test it.

A good example would be a casual hiker deciding to test themselves on a more difficult mountain. By doing this, it takes them out of their comfort zone and also pushes their limits.

The second more figurative loss of flexibility is a loss of spirit. You don't want to lose your playfulness in the process of developing your unshakeable resolve. It is important to remain goofy, silly, and to remember to smile.

Living a serious disciplined life without any jokes is not only dreary, but it is also ineffective. This approach to discipline is more brittle and more prone to psychological problems than discipline interspersed with humour.

People in some of the most difficult professions (miners, sherpas, special forces operators) are known for their constant ribbing and sense of humour. These are some of the toughest people on the planet, but they usually understand that humour is as important as anything else in their line of work.

Remember to laugh, joke, or smile during the most challenging moments. Don't let your pursuit of discipline turn you into a dull humorless person. Instead, let your discipline make you confident enough to make fun of yourself and not take life so seriously.

12. Discipline as an End in Itself

Discipline is often understood as a tool to get the things that you really want. This is because many of the great things in life require self-discipline. Some amount of self-discipline is necessary for success in business, physical fitness, mastery of a skill, great works of art, financial stability, and other desirable accomplishments. Discipline can be thought of as a means to an end, and this is accurate. But, a deeper realization is that discipline is also an end in itself.

When you see discipline as the goal and purpose in your life, you are in complete control of your existential fulfillment. With discipline as the objective, your sense of meaning entirely depends on the choices that you make. On the other hand, when external goals are the end, your existential fulfillment depends on forces outside of your control.

Changing your value system is neither quick nor easy. It is a long process and it may be impossible to completely divorce your self-worth from external achievements. However, discipline as the end goal is an ideal you should strive towards. Moving in that direction will not only increase your control over your sense of meaning, but it will also mean achieving the external goals you had previously focused on.

While financial security certainly eases your nerves, discipline is the most reliable and fulfilling way to find satisfaction and peace of mind. Discipline is the ultimate shield against stress, criticism, and self-doubt. Knowing that you did exactly what you were supposed to do is an impervious armour which sustains you through any uncomfortable environment. Usually, if you are faithful to your discipline, no disappointments in the external world will be able to affect you. Athletes often motivate themselves to train harder because they don't want to leave anything on the table at game day. They know that even if they lose, if they put in their best effort they won't be disappointed by their results. On the other hand, if they slack off in training and almost win the actual match, they may regret their undisciplined choices for years to come. Apply the same approach to your discipline and your life. Never shirk your duties to yourself.

Committing to your quest for more discipline will bless you with all kinds of desirable achievements and a life you didn't realize was possible. These achievements will be rewarding, particularly in the beginning. However, the greatest treasure you will find in living a more disciplined life will be an unshakeable inner peace. Everyone, even self-discipline beginners, can achieve this inner peace right now. For example, if you haven't exercised in years and you go to the gym and perform a safe, but intensive routine. Afterwards you will feel a transcendent level of satisfaction no temptation can deliver. If you keep showing up to the gym, you will strengthen this sense of inner peace. It is important to note that peace is not guaranteed. Even people who have acquired advanced discipline are at risk of losing their inner peace. All it takes is a few undisciplined choices for their calmness to deteriorate. However, regaining peace of mind simply requires returning to the disciplined path. Self-discipline will reward you with the deepest, most profound, and most consistent feelings of meaning, inner peace, and existential satisfaction available to human beings.

A life committed to discipline is not easy; in fact, it may be the most challenging path we can take. Self-discipline shows us that challenges are not something to avoid; rather they are our salvation. By taking the most difficult path we strengthen ourselves and find tranquility in our own minds.

EVAN RAYMER

Bibliography

Baumeister, Roy F., et al. "Ego Depletion: Is the Active Self a Limited Resource?" *Journal of Personality and Social Psychology*, vol. 74, no. 5, 1998, pp. 1252–1265, 10.1037//0022-3514.74.5.1252. Accessed 6 Aug. 2019.

Baumeister, Roy F, and John Tierney. *Willpower: Rediscovering the Greatest Human Strength*. New York, Penguin Books, 2012.

Cal Newport. *Be so Good They Can't Ignore You: Why Skills Trump Passion in the Quest for Work You Love*. New York, Ny, Business Plus, 2012.

---. *DEEP WORK: Rules for Focused Success in a Distracted World*. Place Of Publication Not Identified], Grand Central Pub, 2018.

Clear, James. *Atomic Habits*. Place Of Publication Not Identified], Random House Business, 2017.

Erritzoe, D., et al. "Effects of Psilocybin Therapy on Personality Structure." *Acta Psychiatrica Scandinavica*, vol. 138, no. 5, 19 June 2018, pp. 368–378, 10.1111/acps.12904. Accessed 6 Aug. 2019.

Ferriss, Timothy, and Arnold Schwarzenegger. *Tools of Titans: The Tactics, Routines, and Habits of Billionaires, Icons, and World-Class Performers*. Boston, Houghton Mifflin Harcourt, 2017.

Goggins, David. *Can't Hurt Me: Master Your Mind and Defy the Odds*. United States, Lioncrest Publishing, 2018.

Greene, Robert. *Mastery.* New York, New York, Penguin Books, 2013.

---. *The Laws of Human Nature.* Penguin Usa, 2019.

Harari, Yuval N. *Homo Deus: A Brief History of Tomorrow.* New York, Ny, Harper Perennial, 2018.

Jocko Willink. *Discipline Equals Freedom: Field Manual.* New York, St. Martin's Press, 2017.

Jocko Willink, and Leif Babin. *Extreme Ownership: How U.S. Navy SEALs Lead and Win.* Sydney, N.S.W., Macmillan, 2018.

John Cunningham Lilly. *Programming and Metaprogramming in the Human Biocomputer.* Place Of Publication Not Identified, Crown, 1987.

Jung, C G, et al. *Man and His Symbols.* Bowdon, Cheshire, England] Stellar Classics, 2013.

Jung, C G, and Aniela Jaffé. *Memories, Dreams, Reflections.* London, Fontana, 1993.

Liebenberg, Louis. "Persistence Hunting by Modern Hunter-Gatherers." *Current Anthropology*, vol. 47, no. 6, Dec. 2006, pp. 1017–1026, 10.1086/508695. Accessed 6 Aug. 2019.

Manson, Mark. *Everything Is F*cked: A Book about Hope.* New York, Harper, 2019.

---. *The Subtle Art of Not Giving a Fuck: A Counterintuitive Approach to Living a Good Life.* New York, Ny, Harperluxe, An Imprint Of Harpercollinspublishers, 2018.

Mcgonigal, Kelly. *The Willpower Instinct: How Self-Control Works, Why It Matters, and What You Can Do to Get More of It.* New York, Avery, 2013.

MP, Desai, et al. "Worldwide Trends in Body-Mass Index, Underweight, Overweight, and Obesity from 1975 to 2016: A Pooled Analysis of 2416 Population-Based Measurement Studies in 128.9 Million Children, Adolescents and Adults." *Yearbook of Paediatric Endocrinology*, 11 Sept. 2018, 10.1530/ey.15.13.20. Accessed 6 Aug. 2019.

Newport Cal. *Digital Minimalism*. Random House Usa, 2019.

Pressfield, Steven. *The War of Art*. London, Orion, 2003.

"Robert Sapolsky - Frontal Cortex and Development." *YouTube*, 18 June 2016, www.youtube.com/watch?v=lX74CfRAZmo. Accessed 6 Aug. 2019.

Said-Metwaly, Sameh, et al. "Approaches to Measuring Creativity: A Systematic Literature Review." *Creativity. Theories – Research - Applications*, vol. 4, no. 2, 20 Dec. 2017, pp. 238–275, 10.1515/ctra-2017-0013. Accessed 6 Aug. 2019.

Sala, Giovanni, and Fernand Gobet. "Does Far Transfer Exist? Negative Evidence From Chess, Music, and Working Memory Training." *Current Directions in Psychological Science*, vol. 26, no. 6, 25 Oct. 2017, pp. 515–520, 10.1177/0963721417712760. Accessed 6 Aug. 2019.

Smaers, Jeroen B., et al. "Exceptional Evolutionary Expansion of Prefrontal Cortex in Great Apes and Humans." *Current Biology*, vol.

27, no. 10, May 2017, p. 1549, 10.1016/j.cub.2017.05.015. Accessed 6 Aug. 2019.

Soeliman, Fatemeh Azizi, and Leila Azadbakht. "Weight Loss Maintenance: A Review on Dietary Related Strategies." *Journal of Research in Medical Sciences: The Official Journal of Isfahan University of Medical Sciences*, vol. 19, no. 3, 2014, pp. 268–75, www.ncbi.nlm.nih.gov/pmc/articles/PMC4061651/#ref3. Accessed 6 Aug. 2019.

Vohs, Kathleen, et al. *Decision Fatigue Exhausts Self-Regulatory Resources — But So Does Accommodating to Unchosen Alternatives.* 2005.

"What Does the Brain's Frontal Cortex Do? (Professor Robert Sapolsky Explains)." *YouTube*, 18 Oct. 2017, www.youtube.com/watch?v=3RRtyV_UFJ8. Accessed 6 Aug. 2019.

Yuval Noah Harari. *21 Lessons For The 21St Century.* Place Of Publication Not Identified], Vintage, 2019.

Yuval Noah Harari. *Sapiens: A Brief History of Humankind.* New York Harper Perennial, 2018.

Made in the
USA
Columbia, SC